THE SIDE JOB TOOL BOX

How to: Write a Book, Start a Business Book and Book Marketing Book for Entrepreneurs

Jeffrey W. Bennett M.B.A.

THE SIDE JOB TOOL BOX

How to: Write a Book, Start a Business Book and Book Marketing Book for Entrepreneurs

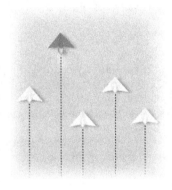

Jeffrey W. Bennett M.B.A.

The Side Job Tool Box - How to: write a book, start a business book and book marketing book for entrepreneurs

Formerly titled: *Get Rich in a Niche*

Published by: Red Bike Publishing

Copyright © 2022 by Jeffrey W. Bennett

Published in the United States of America
www.redbikepublishing.com

ISBN 13: 978-1-936800-37-7
Library of Congress Control Number: 2022933205

ACKNOWLEDGEMENTS

None of this would have been possible without the loving support of my family. Writing and publishing is a time consuming business and you have refreshed me with your limitless patience and unconditional love.

I would like to thank Shama Patel for her social media support and editing services. You can reach her at Evening Light Designs, LLC https://www.eveninglightdesigns.com.

I have a gift for you.

I have a downloadable workbook with all the tables and questions at www.redbikepublishing.com/nicheworkbook

If you are able to, feel free to tell me about how you are going to use your knowledge. You can email me @ editor@redbikepublishing.com.

Contents

CHAPTER 1 WHY THIS BOOK

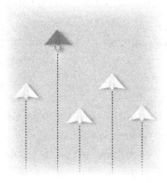

LET'S GO!

Let's get started on building your business. Begin now and learn how to become an expert, write about your expertise, publish your book, and market it. This book will teach you to write and create your very own book, nestled in the industry you have specialized in. If you aren't specialized in a niche yet, you will be if you apply the techniques found in this book. You will soon understand how to write, publish, and sell books to your specialized market. So, I encourage you to read the first three chapters immediately. Don't be discourage by the page count, it's a quick read and full of valuable information that you should be able to apply immediately.

NICHE DEFINED

A niche is simply an area of specialization; this is exactly what your side job tool box should address. These specialized markets may consist of only a few thousand people and may have needs that aren't being directly met by traditional publishers or even industry related products and services. That's where you come in.

Your niche market instructions will require you to address new and refreshing ideas that are far more cutting-edge than you'll find in other marketing books. Working in a niche is trickier than marketing to more generalized audiences. While reading this book, you should be able to apply lessons from successful marketing techniques that I have used but without huge added business costs. Many of these lessons developed through my leadership in the military, M.B.A. studies and applied personal experience while growing my company.

I hope to encourage you to start a book based business with minimal up-front money. Most resources are probably already available to you (computer, Internet provider, and desktop publishing software). Other expenses include some additional up-front publishing costs.

If you already have the basics, then you can begin immediately and develop a great business without going into debt. Start earning money as soon as customers find you.

This book is divided into ten chapters demonstrating where to begin, how to write and publish your book, bring awareness to your products, provide great customer service, and grow the enterprise. This is a book that will help your business age gracefully and give you a consistent return on investment.

A Little Background

Chances are that you are already gainfully employed and are involved with other life matters. You are probably considering following both your dream of writing and owning your own business. In that case, you can further identify what you have a passion for and then do something you love in your professional and personal lives. The same goes for the business you want to start.

How to Determine Your Passion

1. First, conduct a skills inventory. In my case, I developed a list of my

skills and abilities such as reading, helping, designing, running and creating. Conduct a personal inventory and see what you love to do.

2. Next, narrow the list to a few easy-to-manage skills that you can work on and develop. What skill, ability, or personal success really excites you? What do you just love doing that you can spend a lot of time with and you don't even watch the clock? Mine came down to a desire to write and a strong urge to teach. Both of these skills I had learned on the job and through discovering more about myself. Find out what it is and learn to develop and teach that skill to others.

3. Develop a platform. This is the key ingredient. A platform is just another way of identifying the audience, their needs and how your solution addresses their needs. Become the go-to person for that skill and let everyone know about it.

4. Focus on what you learned about yourself. Lack of passion and lack of really knowing what to do will hinder your dreams.

Passion Defined

Using my experience, let me continue:

Passion is hard to define, so I'll draw upon a scene from my earlier experiences.

"I have a great idea that will help other people earn the certification!" I exclaimed to my wife, almost immediately after telling some great news.

"Wait a minute, let's get back to the certification," my wife replied, redirecting the conversation. "You passed the exam?" Her smile demonstrated how happy she was for me.

"Thanks. Sorry about changing the subject," I replied. "I know that you were pulling for me." I hugged my wife one more time before continuing. "It's just that I passed it so easily. It's not that I'm so smart, but I was able to find the answers so quickly and I think I can help other people do it. I can make a difference here."

Can you see the passion? I was onto something. I had written books, attempted to start a few small businesses and was struggling with some new ideas, but nothing had clicked. I knew the reason was lack of passion and not really knowing what I wanted to do. Finally, I was onto something that I could get excited about, teaching people how to study for a certification.

First, let's talk about the message of passion and how I had found it. Not too long ago, I had left a successful career in the Army. While in the service, I had served in intelligence, transportation, and wrapped up my career in recruiting. Prior to my departure from the Army, I read all of the books I could on marketing, sales, interviewing, and resume writing. Almost everything I read revealed the same message: *Find something you are good at and do it.*

Once I left the Army, I spent a few months pondering my future and reading more books. I enrolled in a class on how to start my own business. Aside from learning how to develop business plans, I heard presentations from successful business owners. Again, the message was clear: *Find something you enjoy and do it.* However, this time the message hit home. I met many local business owners who poured all their lives into something they enjoyed.

One business owner stands out from the others; he believes in giving back. As the man stood in front of the class, he explained that business ownership takes a lot of smart work. The owner has to invest resources such as time, self and money. They also must get buy-in from the family. Business entrepreneurs should be able to give and help others succeed. Then, he gave everyone in the class a A fifty dollar bill and recommended two books. Though I won't be handing out fifty dollars anytime soon, I'll give you the names of the books: *The E-myth Revisited* and *Now, Discover Your Strengths*. Both books are powerful and definitely fundamental to learning about how to work on a business (not in the business) and how to know what your strengths are and focus on improving them (not your weaknesses).

In my journey to find the right business, I took a job in defense security. It was fun and I could use my strengths and the transferable skills I had learned in the Army to begin a new niche career. As I learned about my job, I also developed a new goal: to be considered an expert within five years (Figure 1-1). Using Figure 1-1, the "Requirement" column lists what it will take for a person to become an industry or hobby expert. In the example, I knew I needed to develop skills, get more formal education, and become board certified. The "Action" column is used to list activities supporting the requirements. For example, to earn the certification, I planned to form a study group, find a mentor, take on jobs that increased my skills and study books about my profession.

Requirement	Action				
Develop Technical Skills	Study profession	Assume additional tasks	Join professional organization		
Get Degree	Determine degree	Register for college			
Earn Professional Certification	Form study group	Find a mentor	Assume additional tasks related to certification	Study profession	
Brand as an Expert	Develop Internet presence	Write articles	Lead a professional organization	Teach	Write a book

Figure 1-1 5 Year Plan to Become an Expert

I enjoyed the career and began applying my skills to becoming a better employee and checking off steps in my goal to be an expert. I enrolled in an M.B.A. program, taught career classes, joined a professional security organization and began studying for their certification.

Being an expert requires knowledge and demonstration of that knowledge to those who recognized your skill level.

The Evolution of a Business

I felt the need to write this background information to help you better understand my motivation to teach you how to start a business. If you have no idea what you want to do for a business, my experience might help.

In the beginning, I wrote my first security book and marketed for my publishing company Red Bike Publishing at *www.redbikepublishing. com*.

My intent was to teach other security professionals how to study for the exam and maximize their chances of passing. One vital ingredient to this business's success is that there are no other study guides and the certification is new. I began selling an eBook version of the study guide *ISP Certification-The Industrial Security Professional Exam Manual* on my website and eBay.

I started advertising in our professional organization's newsletter and began to draw interest. Sales were limited and after making adjustments in price, they began to escalate. My business plan called for publishing only the eBook to simulate a real test taking environment. However, my customers' feedback led me to change my publishing plan to bring more credibility to the book.

Going to Print

I realized this book needed to be more readily available than on my website. I also began to understand that those in my profession did not want an eBook. I could better help by printing it and listing on *Amazon.com* and other bookstores. I began by writing other niche authors and asking them a lot of questions. Fitting the mold of true entrepreneurs, they volunteered to help me in any way they could and told me their stories. William Henderson, the owner of Last Post Publishing gave me tremendous help. He is a definite success at niche marketing and self-publishing. I used his advice to start Red Bike Publishing, found a printer and distributor to work with, and put it in print.

Sales continued to climb and I learned how to market my product and listened to the market for spin-off product ideas. The journey has been inspiring as I have met others in the business whom I would have not met otherwise. Aside from a good supplemental income, I helped people become certified. I communicate with many of my customers and they frequently send new product ideas, reply to my surveys, and offer advice and support.

Now, I would like to teach you the rest of the lessons. I want to give you the facts and let you experiment on your own business and ideas. What I am about to teach you has been proven over and over and taught in many different venues. I wish you the best of success as you implement these ideas. I also hope you will share your success and become mentors as well.

Vacuums Exist

As I discovered in my profession, there is a system in place for certification: meet the prerequisites, register, take and pass the certification exam. However, the void was huge in the confidence building for potential candidates and marketing to those candidates. Some professional organizations have tremendous programs to help others become certified, but this certification was new and virtually just getting off the ground. I had finally found a way to help.

This book will help you address needs and overcome one major hurdle: to become a recognized expert. People won't recognize you as an expert unless you develop your platform. When you are recognized, people will understand that buying your books will help and when you speak, they should take notes.

Perhaps you have observed a unique need or product that has not been provided. Maybe, like me, you notice that there is a lack of information, study programs, or guidance within a particular industry. You might even have the answers to help people get to where they need to be or reach some sort of professional or personal goal. You can only share this knowledge if you become recognized as an expert. Only then will people come to you for that answer.

Getting Started With Your Business

Begin by asking yourself the following questions:

What is lacking?
How can I help?
Will others be able to understand the plan?
Will others be willing to pay for this knowledge?
Is there anything that I can offer for free to help build credibility (become "go-to" person)?
What are some concrete ways that I can get my message out? (This book will help you find those ways.)

Finding a solution to the void should be relatively simple and the discovery should stir some passion within you. Forcing a product where a need doesn't exist or trying to fill a gap where you don't have expertise will make your task terribly daunting. Filling the vacuum with products that people want and will pay for should be a natural occurrence. The product should be easily recognizable and create a Eureka moment when your target audience finds it.

I Want You to Get the Desired Response

When people find you or your product, they should rave. Comments, recommendations, and praise will probably contain some of the following phrases:

"I was wondering when this would be available."
"I'm surprised I hadn't heard about it earlier."
"I can't wait to get mine."
"Why doesn't _____ (enter name of professional organization or influencer) endorse this product?"
"Why have we not heard about this before?"

These responses are real and have not been coerced, just a natural response to the discovery of long-awaited products. You will also be able to purposefully create and market your product for your audience to easily discover.

I Want You to Become an Expert

As you work to discover how to meet the need, prepare to become a teacher. This could mean anything from instructing at night school, seminars, being a guest speaking or writing articles to gain influence and earn respect as an expert. As you work on your plan, write your book and begin marketing. If you don't already have your book, start writing it. Discover the needs your potential audience might have.

A few years ago I wrote an article on flying for a military magazine. I was in the army and had just earned my private pilots license. The magazine paid me a whopping $600 for the article. That was my first experience with writing.

Next I approached an aviation magazine and offered the same article. They turned me down flat. I couldn't believe it. What was the difference? They had no idea who I was.

In the second example, I was one in a million private pilots clamoring for a voice; why should anyone listen to me?

In the first example, the military magazine paid big bucks for my article because I was a service member trying something new. I was introducing aviation as an "expert" on the topic.

Primarily, you should be able to answer the question: "Who is _(your name here)_ and why should we listen to them?"

I Want You to Prepare for Critics and Challengers

As you rise in popularity as an adviser, expert, and consultant or however you view your position, people will question your motives, knowledge base, and expertise. Be prepared to answer these questions with confidence. For example, as I began to sell more books, some people in the profession took notice of what I was doing. Industry leaders asked whether or not my products were endorsed by the sponsoring professional organization. Others asked about my experience and what gave me the authority to write the books.

Be prepared to welcome those questions with enthusiasm. Your positive and welcoming attitude creates opportunities to sell your product. When people ask questions, it's only because they need good answers before entrusting or allowing you to be their adviser. Be thankful for these objections, because many more people will pass you by without even asking. They may just assume that you either are or are not qualified and be unwilling to emotionally commit to your product.

Being fortunate enough to answer the questions will allow a chance to defend your position. Additionally, when they buy into your teachings, they will recommend you to their colleagues. Always look for ways to make allies during the most challenging of situations.

There are too many professionals who become easily insulted when their credentials are called into question; don't become one of those. I know of one occasion where a client asked a professional organization representative why they should be certified. The representative became indignant and flustered that someone would ask such a question. They moved on without even encouraging the client to become certified.

Their pride had overcome their mission: to get people professionally certified. As a leader, you should establish credibility and be able to defend that credibility with the emotional ties to your clients. Then your clients will allow you to take them on the journey.

I Want You to Market at the Right Place and Time

Traditional marketing may or may not work when operating in a niche environment. Because of the limited audience, marketing efforts should be targeted and intense. Your market may or may not have open lines of communication, you may not be able to define your audience demographically, you may not have easy access to a combined or complete mailing list, and you may not be able to blast advertisement to the precise people who need to see it.

Professional organizations may be too small for large marketing organizations to be able to spend time and money to reach, and the effort may be too expensive for the return on investment. They are used to representing broader markets and having mailing lists that can be used for different applications. In that case, don't employ these marketing organizations; you may have more fun creating your own opportunities. For example, they may have a list to reach a certain demographic. That demographic is willing to buy cars, books, music, televisions, and so on. However, finding a specific customer base that wants to learn how to protect sensitive products, study the secrets of snails, or the fine art of making egg jewelry is going to be extremely difficult.

Your expensive marketing campaign may reach one hundred thousand, five hundred thousand, or five hundred million depending on how much you invest, but are you sure it is going to reach the three thousand decision makers in your niche market? If you do get a purchase response, does your demographic audience have the purchasing power to allow you to recapture your expense? Probably not. You've just invested time and money on hope; not a good business strategy. I'll show you how to target your search and get your message to those who need it.

I Want You to Write Your Book

Books are an excellent and inexpensive way to reach your target and launch your business. Readers regard authors as experts. Whenever an author writes, is quoted, or publishes, people tend to lend credibility. The pen is mighty and powerful in launching careers and products.

Your book could be about you, your product or solely your message. Whatever the subject matter, the book should highlight your expertise in an area, your message, and any related products.

Why write a book? Some of the following purposes may help you find the answer:

You have a message no one else has made known.
You are an expert in a field where no books exist (highly possible in a niche).
You know how to do something that you wish everyone else in the niche could do.
You want to build instant credibility.
You want to change an industry practice.

Successful authors have written to meet some or all of the above personal and professional goals. I wrote my book Red Bike Publishing's *Unofficial Study Guide For: ISP Certification-The Industrial Security Professional* because I had passed a test that many others feared to take. Our field has well over ten thousand eligible professionals, but only a hundred were certified at the time. I wanted to demonstrate to others that though they may already have the required experience and know how, I could lead them to hurdle the confidence obstacle. I wanted to take the mystery out of how to study for and take the examination and instill confidence that moved professionals to certify. This book launched even more books, including *DoD Security Clearance and Contracts Guide Book, Insider's Guide to Security Clearances,* and more.

What's your message? Do you have a burning desire to instill confidence? Do you want something changed and are you able to articulate the path to change? Can you help someone improve their professional standing? If so, you may be ready to write and publish *The Insider's Guide to: (your subject here)*. Later, we'll show you exactly how to do that.

Writing a book isn't easy and shouldn't be something an author rushes through, no matter what pop publishing culture tells us. What goes on paper is a result of tireless effort. Depending on your motivation and personality, it may seem easier to put together a course or write an article or two for a newsletter, blog, or other publication.

Here are four proven ways to help you write and publish in a specialized market and establish yourself as a niche expert.

1. Writing takes time

Writing a book-length manuscript is difficult and requires commitment. It takes time, devotion, and some solitude, much of which a full time professional does not have in abundance. This endeavor is not a sprint, but an endurance race. The difficulty of formatting a book may not be as tough as setting aside time and committing to writing words on paper.

As a future author/publisher, you have already identified niches that aren't supplied by other publications. The market is hungry for knowledge, but to date, no book has been supplied. On the other hand, there might be a book or two published, but there is room for others.

2. Start with quality over quantity

As an author, you are not necessarily writing to beat others to market, but to get a champion product that meets a need. It also may be a good assumption that as you write, you will remain as the sole source expert on the topic. Until you succeed, others may not even have the energy or desire to write about your subject area. Once you succeed, others may join you in the market.

3. You are the sole provider

Remember, your niche could be too small for traditional publishers to venture into. Even if all the customers bought books, there wouldn't be enough sales to warrant the huge financial, time, and resource commitment required of a traditional publisher. This is a great opportunity because your market is protected. In business, we measure it as barriers to entry. You have a built-in audience with no competition; that's called demand.

As an example, I marketed my first book to a traditional publisher. I explained that the size of my market is about twenty thousand professionals. They passed on the book explaining the market was too small and they would lose money. Wow, what if I sell twenty thousand of my books? That's a lot of dough. You can meet your niche in the same way.

4. Shovel ready audience

All you have to do is commit to the project, organize your thoughts, complete a manuscript, edit the manuscript, and publish it. There are many methods for publishing. What I recommend in these pages does not involve getting your book in bookstores, signing with major publishing companies or a model involving a lot of wasted effort trying to replicate traditional publishing or marketing strategies. The premise: you are writing for a niche, so focus on what works specific to your niche.

I Want You to Create Spin off Products

Your book doesn't have to be the only product. In fact, a book may be the door to more business. Follow-on books, products, training programs, speaking engagements, consulting, and other opportunities may spring from your book. These products may already exist before the book. In that case, a book is an opportunity to expand your market and increase your influence.

Remember how your favorite TV shows spawned other shows that involved costars? These were often referred to as spin-offs. Spin-off products are additional offerings that are spawned by your core product. This should be not forced, but a natural progression. They should develop out of a relationship between you, your product and customers. The flow doesn't necessarily have to be in that order, but the relationship should be easy enough for you and the customer both to ask, "What's next?" When you develop products, you and the customers may experience yet another Eureka moment.

The good thing about this relationship is that unless your product crosses other niche boundaries, you may not need to do any additional marketing. Your book marketing will help you sell your spin-off products. As you market your books, include the catalog of other products. Your product store or listings could mention "from the author of _____". Include all of your books and products on the last page of each publication. You can see an example at the end of this book.

Hopefully, as you continue to read this book, you'll be thinking of this symbiotic marketing strategy and not only find ideas for books, but also for some of the likely spin-off products that may result from your book or other core products. In fact, if your products existed before your book, they may provide anecdotes or other success stories of how you or your products have helped people in the industry.

I want you to Have Follow-On Products

Sales happen when you have a good product and strategy, a completed book, and spin-off products. What next? Why not another book and more spin-off products? The opportunities for success may continue to manifest and you may find yourself ready to quit your day job. Some remarkable experiences may come up that provide new ideas for you to grow as a professional and offer additional messages to your customers and potential new customers. Wouldn't it be nice to be able to maintain newly created momentum from your writing and marketing?

Remain open to new ideas, but stay focused on reality. Several people have contacted me about other great opportunities. One offered a nice salary to join his organization part time. I was flattered, but it required travel and would take me away from what I love doing. Enticing opportunities will come up; just make sure they line up with your goals and capabilities.

I hope you can see the vision and be motivated to action. Sure, you are working in a small niche that perhaps others can't afford to work in.

You are the one who has labored for hours and invested money and time in the niche and now someone is advising you to leave this comfort zone and take on a new role; well, not exactly. What I am suggesting should be a next step in the progression of your business. You've spent your efforts in a particularly small subject, and have learned some valuable transferable skills. Why not share them?

Summary

I hope to teach you how to identify and meet a need using a sound and targeted niche marketing strategy. This is meant to modify traditional marketing and cut out unproductive advertising efforts. This will require some unique thinking skills and creativity enough to reach a fickle target audience. Are you ready to do this?

Review Questions

Considering your Skills

1. Brainstorm and document a list of skills, talents, and strengths.

a.

b.

c.

d.

e.

f.

g.

h.

2.   Narrow that list down to a few that are easy to manage and are most enjoyable. Which skills have you been celebrated for?

3.   From that list, what do you love to do so much that you lose yourself in the moment?

4.   Name five things related to the list that you can teach or write about.

a.

b.

c.

d.

e.

5.   What organizations or persons can you list as possible customers, readers, or students?

a.

b.

c.

d.

Considering Your Industry:

1.   What education is lacking?

2.   How can you help?

3.   How can you help others understand the plan?

4.   Will others be willing to pay for this knowledge?

5.   What can you offer for free to help build my credibility (become "go-to" person)?

6.   What are some concrete ways that you can get the message out?

7.   What's your message?

8.   How can I satisfy my burning desire to instill confidence?

9.   What changes can you make and are you able to articulate the path to change?

10. How can you help someone improve their professional standing?

CHAPTER 2 BUSINESS DEVELOPER SKILLS

Introduction

You have ideas, skills and hobbies that you can write about and develop into a thriving business. You have found a gap in a system, service, education or other product and want to provide a solution. Many of these gaps are so small that larger organizations just aren't able to see them; that's where you fit in.

This chapter focuses on how you can become influential in your industry and develop a foundation for your business. You may be well known, or merely taking the first steps to establishing yourself as an authority. This chapter can help you identify the strengths necessary to meet your goals and establish a successful teaching and writing career.

Niche experts

An entrepreneur in a small niche market can provide solutions with little cost. Because you have the right skills, you can do so much with little cost and risk. Writing a book, and publishing either yourself or through other non-traditional alternatives is a real possibility. Because you know what needs to be written and who will buy it, you will be able to inform and provide your target market with valuable resources with little difficulty. Most likely, you are already a busy professional and possibly involved with career, family, and several volunteer organizations. Now you have a burning desire to fulfill this dream on top of everything else. Well, it's definitely possible.

What makes this book different is that it is written with the understanding that you may already have a full time job, and potentially a great reputation. One thing to avoid is becoming one of those annoying professionals who, while at their day job, make hard sales, talk constantly about their side business, wave books in everyone's faces, or sell to subordinates. It might just ruin your reputation and get you fired.

However, you can use your book as an opportunity to help others; demonstrating your expertise. I'll show you how to focus on what you can control and make a good income while you are at it. As a professional, you have a code of ethics to live by. What you do will often affect your reputation.

In niche publishing, your goal might be to become sort of a celebrity expert. Build upon the expertise by helping others, and the book sales will follow. I know this because I am possibly one of the worst face-to-face salespersons ever. I believe in my product, but because of conflicting life roles, I find it difficult to go through the requirements to make direct sales. I worry about seeing my bosses at conventions, seeing peers at professional luncheons, and being penalized for using company time to sell my product. That gives me only after work hours and vacation time to present and sell face-to-face.

This book will assist you with developing a writing, publishing, sales and marketing plan that allows you to be yourself, protect your professional status and provide a great service.

An entrepreneur in a small niche market can provide solutions with little cost. Because you have the right skills, you can do so much with little cost and risk. The following are useful elements for writing a book and publishing either yourself or through other non-traditional alternatives:

- A great book idea that needs to be developed
- An identified customer base
- Methods to inform and provide your target market with valuable resources
- Ability to balance career, family and other commitments

So, remembering that you are a professional with a full time job, how can you possible market to the people that you might already have a business relationship paid for by your current boss?

It may be possible as long as you don't use company resources or time, but make sure; you don't want to get fired. For example, suppose you are employed full time as a mid-level safety supervisor. You also are very active in an Occupational Safety and Health Administration related professional organization. You have discovered an incredible way to help people become better safety managers and increase safety awareness. You write a book, publish a newsletter, and start a little side business.

If you follow the latest trends of marketing and sales techniques, you might do so to your professional detriment as you become a nuisance to fellow professionals. Instead of becoming a person of influence in the safety industry, you are considered an aggressive sales person and one to be avoided. Even worse, you get a reputation for doing so on "company time." So, how do you balance a professional reputation while building your personal business empire?

For those of you who already run your businesses full time, you can employ book-selling strategies that will get your book noticed without you becoming a distraction. You can provide a great book with a certain amount of anonymity mixed with a little niche popularity without gaining a reputation that could harm your other accomplishments. You do so by helping: offering a valuable product that is not otherwise provided.

You might feel the same way. So, how do you create such an opportunity?

Establish a strong online presence that brings your potential customers to you. By doing so, your brand can become synonymous with your industry. Potential customers will see you as an industry expert with real solutions serving your niche. But if you do it wrong, you will be perceived as an opportunist.

I'll explain how to sell books within your niche by leveraging your reputation, expertise, and ability to fill an educational void. When people hear of you, they will already know about your book. You will also learn how to overcome tough situations as you work with professional and hobbyist organizations.

Entrepreneurs

This book is for those of you with an entrepreneurial spirit. You see a problem and offer a solution that is accurate, to the point, and both affordable and valuable to the consumer. You have ideas that work and implement those ideas. Because of the need, the flow of the idea and relation to the customer should be natural. Your passion for your subject motivates you to work beyond what you normally might give to your employer, and your priorities have shifted somewhat to accommodate this desire.

Entrepreneurs are often known for great wealth and overcoming incredible odds to become successful. We celebrate their success in magazines and television shows. However, they are only a small demographic. In fact, there are many more who have created businesses that fill small specific needs that may accomplish much in their specialty, but because of the small niche, will never rise to superstar status (outside of the niche). Though not celebrated publicly, these incredible people have created careers while solving problems for their small niche. They may not have employees, but they fill critical needs with products and services.

Bright

It takes brains to figure out a solution and make it affordable, valuable, and appealing to a particular customer. Identifying the customer may be simple, but reaching them requires brilliance. An identifiable demographic for your niche may not exist, but you can change that. In this case, you should focus efforts on associating your name with your expertise. Similarly, you may have already created a built-in market through social, professional, or hobbyist networks. Your strategy will be demonstrating your solutions; your customers will be grateful that you reached them, and so will you.

Bright also applies to the ability to communicate well enough to write your manuscript. It may seem easy to put words down on paper, but quite another thing when trying to create an emotional response and call to action. You know what your message is, but how will you communicate it?

Thick Skin

Writing to a niche market proves difficult when a technical know-it-all offers her critiques. While others are hungrily feeding on your wisdom and teachings, there are some who will contest your choice of wording, motivation, or other issues. They are the purists who may argue when you open up new ways of thinking and solving problems. In a niche market, you may create solutions that go against traditional thinking. That's why you are needed, because you are smart enough to think and offer solutions.

When I began writing for the industrial security community,

I provided services, products, and books that were helping the profession. I knew I had the right solution based on positive feedback and praise on *Amazon.com*. People were more than glad to let me know how much I had helped them. They also complimented me on some more nontraditional solutions. Likewise, when you help others, they respond in kindness and the world is a better place…well, almost.

There were some who questioned my experience, my writings, and my motivations. Reviews had nothing to do with the content of the book and included some unsavory comments about my motivation. This is where thick skin comes in.

So, how do you handle this kind of publicity? Embrace it. After all, comments open doors and can be free publicity. At the very least, it creates a buzz. In reality, the market decides whether or not you are a success, not the critics.

The smaller your niche, the more resistance you might meet. This resistance may be strong at first, but will weaken as your book gets to customers. Again, the market determines success or failure. Changing the status quo way of thinking is sometimes difficult, and that's why problem solvers are so valuable.

The only metrics that count are whether or not you are reaching your target and whether or not your audience is buying your books. While others are ranting, your books are selling. Keep this success in mind. Reflect on the results of the good you are doing, and not on the comments of a select few who might be experiencing professional envy.

Your thick skin could also provide a way to meet people's objectives. Perhaps some of your critics do not even understand your message. Or, maybe your message could be improved. I published a second book called *How to Get US Government Contracts and Classified Work* for a focused group of security managers. The book is an explanation of government regulations and their implementation in a security policy. Experts from the field with many more years of experience have reviewed the manuscript. Since they have a lot of experience, I value their input.

I had originally intended on publishing the book with a traditional trade publisher. However, they sent the book out to a test market of the wrong group and it wasn't received well. Many criticized the book, not offering help or advice, and many offered conflicting opinions. I could have taken their criticisms personally, but decided to try to learn something from their comments. I tried to see my message from their points of view and soon began to see some constructive avenue for their comments.

I realized they were not my target audience. I eventually pulled the project and published it with my newly formed publishing company. I found my target market and since then, the book has become a consistent go to book within my profession.

Politician

Amazon.com is filled with book reviews unrelated to the book's content. What you should seek in your manuscript and books is sincere reviews and comments.

I want to help you be prepared for that possibility with your book. Even with the purest of intentions and motivations, you will face public criticism. A very small but vocal group may not appreciate your work and could attack it from the jealous point of view. They won't offer constructive review, but you may be able to glean some insight from their comments. Be sure your facts are solid. Seek to understand comments and points of view to make a book project much better.

In the face of unsubstantiated comments, you should be able to evaluate your performance by asking: Am I selling books? Has any bad publicity caused a drop in sales?

Friendly

Always be friendly. Create positive and fair reviews when speaking or writing of others and their products. If you can't give a good review, don't give one. Trying to bolster your success while knocking a competitor is bad form and will be viewed that way. Always praise others publicly, but offer constructive criticism privately. Once you say or write a negative comment, it will be hard to take it back no matter how hard you try.

Whenever possible, help everyone. As an expert in your niche, you are the person to field questions to and ask advice of. If at all possible, answer those questions. You may begin to receive email, blog comments and other methods of contact. Answer all of them. Three of my favorite mentor authors always answered my questions; that's why they are my favorites.

If you can't answer the questions, respond that you are not able to answer them but are willing to provide an answer at a later date. Or just let them know you appreciate the question, but it is outside of your experience. Perhaps you could even refer them to a colleague. They'll understand that even in a small niche, you can't be a master of all knowledge. In fact, you will have done a favor for a colleague or fellow vendor by providing a referral. They may want to return the favor.

Always smile while in public and go out of your way to make the customer feel good. I learned this lesson the hard way. Once while setting up a booth at a conference, I provided free books for a door prize. I had requested to have the books awarded at the end of the conference after everyone had a chance to register at my booth for the drawing. Unfortunately, the event organizers had given out my books too early and left me without the benefit of collecting contact information during the registration process. Even more unfortunate, I accidentally expressed my dissatisfaction in front of the person who had won my book. I shudder to think of the embarrassment I had caused the winner, not to mention stealing their joy. What do you think she might be saying to her friends and a new string of possible customers?

Dealing with negative people

Earlier, I wrote about having thick skin. Though critics may give bad reviews or professional organizations may not grant your books favorable coverage, be friendly. Never, ever, EVER return a bad review for a bad review. Treat people with respect and offer professional courtesy. This does not mean be a pushover. Respect means respond to unfair criticism professionally; you may just earn a new and influential customer.

How do you handle unfair issues in a friendly manner? Privately, so there is room to hopefully resolve a misunderstanding without causing embarrassment to either party. Always leave room for an easy resolution.

Take a look at a real event that I recently became aware of. Linda, a professional in a niche industry, paid a professional organization to post an advertisement in the organization's newsletter about a book she had written. The newsletter editor put a disclaimer under her ad stating that the organization did not endorse her product. It seemed like a fair disclaimer until she realized it was only posted with her advertisement. The other vendors had received no such disclaimer.

She decided to write a letter of inquiry about the disclaimer. Before doing so, she researched the organization's by-laws and pointed out that they stated that disclaimers should be posted in a neutral location so that it would apply to all advertisers. She was able to demonstrate in a positive way that the organization applied an unfair practice by singling out her company. Both parties were open to a resolution and have quickly made progress. Had she lashed out, she may have earned a resolution, but possibly with a loss of professional bearing.

The same is true of book reviews. You might receive some bad comments. Fair or not, they stay with you. Take the high road, and don't address them. You'll never win. Learn from the reviews if you can, and just move on.

How else can you handle bad reviews? Bury them under positive reviews. Contact all of your allies in your industry and have them review your book. Don't ask them to provide undeserved good reviews. However, ask them not to review if they cannot post a positive one. Simply provide them with free copies of the book and ask them to review it on *Amazon.com*. Also ask if they will post the review on social networking sites. The positive buzz will overshadow a few negative ones.

Focused

Authors who work in a niche market should maintain focus on their goals. Your efforts are only successful when you get the desired results. To get rich in a niche, you have to make sales. Meeting and greeting is nice and it has its benefits, but sales count. Learn how to protect your time and do what is critical to attract your market and entice customers to buy. It's not easy to convince others that you are the expert. However, the niche marketer should not be easily distracted. The market is so small and every move counts. Intense focus means not giving up when:

The wrong marketing efforts don't work-You may have to create your own marketing plan and even that may not always succeed. The marketing plan should be flexible and have a backup in place when you miss the mark. Contact information may be hard to come by. Keep trying different ways to get contact information. Keep trying new ways of identifying your specific market from the crowd of faces. You want your efforts to attract buyers or influencers.

Writing ideas might come slow-You've got to be committed to getting the message out regularly and in a timely fashion. Blogs, newsletters, and posts on social network sites help get your message out. Go too long without input and people begin to forget about you. You want to stay in the front of your customers' thoughts. If they don't remember you, they won't buy from you or refer you to others.

Sales might begin to wane-You have peak months and then some may turn out to be unproductive. You might want to sit it out and see what happens next, but that would jeopardize your sales. It's important to understand why sales are declining and prepare for such events. Are your articles on point? Has your website lost positioning on Google? Have other niche-related books exceeded your success on Amazon?

When you are dialed into your goal, all of your time is effortlessly committed to reaching it. This requires a good plan with measurable milestones. Without an agenda, you may wander off the successful path and become quickly lost and tangled up in a jungle of ineffective actions.

For example, if you know that going to a professional seminar will produce leads for your newsletter or products, then go with the goal in mind of introducing yourself and collecting as many business cards as possible. If you are setting up a booth to sell books, then your goal may be to hold discussions of the benefit of your books and products and get a response. Both examples can easily become expensive failures if you do not engage potential customers in the right call-to-action activities. Wasting time at the buffet table or engaging in nonproductive conversations is the sign of a lack of a plan.

Creative

Your market may not be easily identifiable, ideas that capture your target's imagination may be elusive, and your audience may be difficult to sell to, but at least you are creative. You have a passion for your niche subject and that alone allows you to demonstrate key characteristics of the creative author and entrepreneur.

Think of the third alternative

Creative people are capable of meeting objectives and striking an emotional response in their customers. In the face of objections or a difficult industry, you are able to overcome your market's negative responses with some very good reasons to say yes. If your audience just can't grasp a tough concept you are presenting, you won't be distracted. You'll be able to present an alternate way of thinking to help walk them through a thought process that takes them out of their comfort zone and into your way of thinking. Your website and product descriptions will encourage them to either spend their own or request corporate funds on your products, even if you are new and haven't yet built a solid reputation.

Have a Message

That passion is a burning message that screams, "I can help make your life easier" or "How do you live without me?" Such a message should be yours exclusively and available everywhere and trustworthy. It doesn't have to reflect the current practices or industry standard to be accepted. You might be considered a revolutionary, and that's okay as long as you are accurate, factual, and not contrary to laws or regulations. It just means that you will have to have a few allies to help preach the soundness of your message.

How do you get your message out? You can talk to everyone you see, present in conferences, and write articles for blogs, newsletters, and social networking sites. Finally, you write a book as the undisputed authority in the subject. A great way to get your message out is to be the first in your industry to press. However, don't rush to get to market at the expense of your message's accuracy or at risk of a poorly edited work. You'll want to be credible on the first printing.

I wrote *ISP and ISOC Master Exam Prep* to help others pass a test composed of questions from a government regulation. All of my venues (speaking, articles, posts and so on) are not entirely about my book, but the regulation. The message has launched my company's publishing of the regulation in book form and spin-off products related to the policy. My message is also transferable to other disciplines and niches. As of this writing, I am contributing to a major online magazine that will expose my message to one hundred thousand more people, and I get paid for it. I no longer write query letters; editors send requests to me. Find a way to make your niche message fit a broader audience.

If you have a strong message, be on the lookout for coaching opportunities. I've held a few seminars for the certification program related to my book and had great sales opportunity. I've also created a continuing education course at the local university where my books are required as part of the curriculum.

Summary

This chapter has focused on characteristics required of an industry expert. It takes hard work, determination, and audacity to teach and write. Having traits of an entrepreneur or politician, displaying friendliness, thick skin, focus, and creativity, and having a message will propel you to the top in your field. Many will be grateful for your contributions, recognizing that you have provided a helpful solution where none had existed before.

REVIEW QUESTIONS

1. From your list of talents, what great book idea needs to be developed?

2. What is the identified customer base that you've developed to sell your book to?

3. Think of ways to inform and provide your target market with valuable resources. (If you can't think of any, more ideas are coming your way in later chapters.)

4. To avoid future conflicts, criticisms, or quarrels, what alliances should you develop or what issues should you resolve with industry, professional, or hobby organizations as you write the book?

CHAPTER 3 IDENTIFY YOUR NICHE

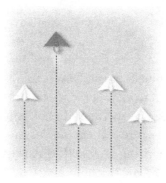

INTRODUCTION

After reading this chapter, you'll know how to provide a service that is in demand. In fact, specialized markets are perfect opportunities to introduce products without having to borrow money or put down large amounts of cash. And, you can make money almost immediately.

The great news is that, because of the challenges of traditional publishing, the audience's demands are valid, but the supply isn't there. That's where you come in, tapping a market with plenty of room to grow. Specialized markets are hurting for experts who are easily accessible and know how to communicate.

NICHE DEFINED

Before we go any further with writing, publishing, and marketing your book and products, we should first identify what a niche is. A niche is a specialized market and is a focused, exclusive discipline. For example, you might find the topic of travel as a niche idea. However, the idea can be fully developed with airline, rail, automobile, and ocean liner subgroups. Niches provide perfect opportunities for you, the teacher, developer, entrepreneur, author or expert. Becoming an expert in a niche is easier and standing out as an expert is just a matter of marketing your skills and abilities.

Types of Niches

Specialized markets are more abundant and successful than many may realize. Traditional publishing models focus marketing on popular and large topics, which work well for general interests. However, many of the suggested marketing methods do not help with identifying and reaching specialized interests. There is value in specialized business and you can become a rising star. In the following pages are examples of some niches and how you might be able to fit in, rise to the top and develop a solid career. There are myriad opportunities to write and publish information about your specialized area of influence and expertise.

Niches attract engaged individuals. Where there is a group of engaged individuals, there is structure. Where there is structure, there is a need for development of standards, products to meet the niche market needs and a way to enjoy the supporting products. Before dedicating time and effort in a niche market, you should ensure a few things are in place.

Desire

You have a passion for the topic; it's hard to succeed in something you neither believe in nor like. One fascinating revelation is the natural progression of relationships. So before you invest a lot of time and funds into supporting a niche, be sure you are committed to the task. A good test is to determine whether or not you could lose track of time while being happily engaged in the work, and, all the while, your heart races, you become excited, and spin-off ideas flow freely.

Become an expert

You should also be the recognized expert. If you have the passion but are not yet confident in the ability to teach, then study, engage other enthusiasts, learn from a mentor and interact daily. Become a full-time student, write about what you learn, journalize progress and be confidently prepared to share your knowledge. Give frequently and make friends and valuable relationships that will help influence others to join you when you finally become an expert. When you are ready to write, teach and engage in intelligent conversation with people in the specialized market; they will already recognize you as the expert.

When you're recognized as an expert, people seek you for information. For example, suppose you belong to a train enthusiast club. You have joined an organization and have access to trains and information related to steam locomotives.

Pretty soon you've taken tours, put together scrapbooks of pictures and writings, and developed a blog and website. Now you might be an enthusiast and an expert. However, you don't know about electric, diesel, or other types of trains. That's okay; your efforts should focus on what you can bring to other steam train enthusiasts. Though train enthusiast groups are a niche, there are specialized subgroups. In Figure 3-1, we see the niche header Train Enthusiast, subgroup Steam Locomotive with the additional subgroups of those steam locomotives retired to museums and those still pulling tours through state parks. Electric Trains are further broken down into Bullet Trains. There is no end to subgroups as long as there is a potential audience.

Develop a product

The next challenge for the train enthusiast is to develop products and services that those in the steam train industry can use and enjoy. Maybe you have a knack for stories, pictures, a unique collection or a way to manufacture models or sculptures. Whatever your talent and skill, you can use them as a medium for sharing your expertise with the steam engine enthusiast world.

Define your market

This is where you find those who share your enthusiasm. From our

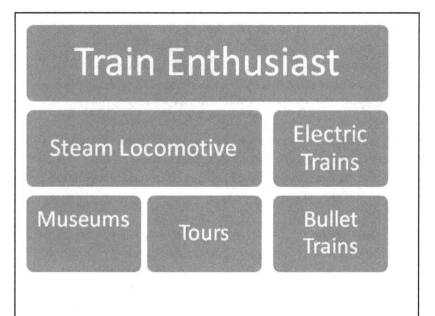

Figure 3-1 Niche Topic with related sub-topics. A niche expert can work in a broad specialty or drill down to reach a more focused market.

steam train example, you can use your favorite search engine to discover museums and transportation businesses where products are sold or create opportunities to speak at steam train enthusiast clubs. You can also write articles for online magazines and research the amount of times the articles were accessed, read, and forwarded. I will show you those techniques later.

One of the necessary components of being successful anywhere is to network and market. For publishing, the buzzword is platform. The good news for niche authors and publishers is that you can establish yourself as an expert, market, network, and build a platform at the same time. These are all interconnected and do not stand alone.

There is no easier or faster opportunity to build your own empire than while addressing niche topics. Specialized markets have ready-made groups that, once established, serve as a captive audience. When your marketing is successful, you'll have a gathering of people who identify with you and your brand.

Lack of literature on subjects

Outside of general subject non-fiction, there may not be books or published articles on your specific niche. Not everyone can write and many publishing companies aren't willing to tackle smaller markets. If there is existing literature on the subject, it will be directed toward the larger, general audience.

Finding a Niche

So, how do you break into the sub-niche or smaller specialized areas? Using the topic of security as an example, we can see how to divide the niche into subcategories. There are lots of books on the subject of security. Popular topics include introduction to security, computer security, information security, national security and many other broad scopes.

However, there are few books written on the subject of protecting proprietary data or how to become the best security guard ever. Every company would love to keep their proprietary information secret, but the topic hasn't been boiled down into a set of procedures applicable to each type of company. There are tens of thousands of security guards, but not many have broached the subject of guarding their post. Do you see how you might be able to fill in an information gap in published literature?

Now, let's look at a few niches and some solutions. This exercise might prove helpful in helping you identify your specialty area and how you can help. Take a look at some topics and see if you can find your niche.

Pets

Products and services for pets continue to be huge business. Even during times of recession, people continue to pamper their pet friends with specialized food, toys, and health products. This market is easy to find given the wealth of magazines, books, and information available. Maybe you have a unique way of caring for your furry, fluffy or feathery friend or have witnessed the special bond between pets and children that hasn't been addressed. The pets niche can be sub-categorized by type or product design.

Some subcategories or specialty areas for pets can be broken down to dogs, cats, exotic animals, fish, birds, and much more. Each category has its own blend of traits and needs. Each subcategory can also be broken down into product and service type. All pets need food, most pets need exercise, toys, health products, recreation and boarding considerations. For example, fish need aquarium accessories, and dogs use chew toys and leashes and need to be cleaned up after they do their business.

Concierge service

Large organizations should concentrate on their core competencies. Without that focus on what they do best, they could expend time and effort in areas that are contrary to goals and mission. Many companies outsource catering, event planning and other client and employee centered needs. Concierge services are springing up to help meet those needs in a big way.

Concierge services also play a big role with tours and events. They welcome new residents, give information about the neighborhood, and provide gift baskets. Personal shoppers fall into the concierge category.

Many in the concierge industry are hungry for ways to market their product and reach potential customers. Some may need ideas and guidance on expanding their services. Can you design a service app or fill gift baskets? Do you know of ways to provide pamphlets, discount gasoline or make inexpensive catered dishes? How about planning for meetings or parties? Maybe you don't want to start a concierge service, but you are bursting with fresh ideas on how to impress clients and employees with the best parties ever. If so, you might just be the one to provide this know-how in books to a competitive and growing niche market.

Security

Recent events have led to heightened security worldwide. School shootings, terrorism, kidnappings, theft, computer hacking and more have led to a growth of security related cottage industries. Security itself is a niche that can be explored deeper. There are several professional organizations ranging from just a few to tens of thousands of members. One of the larger organizations is made up of groups involved in risk management, loss prevention, information protection, and several other security disciplines.

Security professionals are hungry for knowledge. There are great opportunities for writing and providing products and services. Security guards, port, transportation, homeland and various government security functions have audiences with large growth potential. Executive protection and event security is a growing business designed to protect celebrities and fans alike. Computer security is evolving to counter cyber threats world-wide. If you have unique skills and an ability to teach security-related material, there are plenty of professional and organizational disciplines in which to contribute.

Safety

Safety is a regulated and growing industry. Workplace injuries, product recalls, injury compensation, and lawsuits are just a few examples of how integrated consideration for life and health is. Whether laws are federal, civil or personal in nature, we are all responsible for obeying them and providing environments of reduced risk to life and limb.

Safety is a broad field with many consultants and practitioners in various industries. However, this category can be separated into much smaller specialized industries. Occupational Safety and Health Administration (OSHA) provides a large volume regulation that can be managed in small chunks. Electricity, water, welding, walking surfaces, construction, motors and reporting are all subject to OSHA oversight. A knowledgeable person could excel in any area. For example, if you've been welding or teaching welding for many years, you may just have what it takes to build your platform and write on the subject of welding safety. Whole industries that either have a small welding requirement or are totally devoted to nothing but welding are all potential customers. A hot topic today would be mine and oil rig safety. An expert in these areas pretty much has the world's attention.

Home safety is another big industry with a very broad audience. Families with small children and new babies, hobbyists, home businesses and others are interested in making their home sweet home a home safe home. The market is perfect for experts with good ideas for childproofing electrical outlets or choosing which cribs are safest.

Professional organization certification

Perhaps you belong to a professional organization that has a certification. You may have an opportunity to provide a study guide or a book about how to get the certification. If you are good at taking tests and know how to teach others to prepare for tests, you may just have a new career cut out for you. Also, consider how you studied for, wrote a paper, or otherwise performed and passed the certification requirements. Perhaps you've developed a unique skill in that area and have a passion for helping others over this professional hurdle. Where others pass the requirements and move on, the rest are left to fend for themselves. You can help these forgotten clients pass the test.

Don't teach your potential audience to cheat the requirements. It is more noble to show them how prepare, not how to work a system. For example, maybe the test is automated. You might instruct them on the mechanics of test taking. Maybe the test is open book; you might just be able to offer advice on how to search for the answers. If the test is based on writing a paper, you can provide ideas and ways to research information and provide an intelligent and worthy product.

The simple things you found easy might just be valuable education for others. We all have different talents, skills, and abilities. You can use yours to help others along the way. Certifications are abundant in fields such as Security, Human Resources, Accounting, Program Management, Purchasing, Culinary Arts and much more. Even government agencies are developing and requiring certification.

Books about certification tend to make good sales and the authors and publishers can expect to charge a significantly higher price than with a typical trade book. And the certification books have staying powers as long as the certifications are available. I've researched several certifications offered by various professional organizations and many do not have study resources.

I am constantly searching to author other certification books. So many are out there and many lack quality. One existing study guide consists of scanned reports with a fancy cover slapped on it. I think there may be more to offer this group. Maybe you have discovered similar situations where you can help.

Import/Export

There are many careers and specialized professional opportunities in international trade. Countries provide goods and services that other nations crave. Law, economics, logistics, and treaties all play a part in getting goods and services across international borders. Some goods are controlled by international laws. Licenses, agreements, and other permissions must be completed before trade of certain technologies can begin. If you are a niche expert in this area, you may have a specialized market ready to learn and grow. Though the market may be growing in the number of consultants, lawyers, professional organizations, and compliance officers, there are few non-government publications. If you have expertise in this area, there is room for growth as laws, treaties, and policy is ever changing.

Outsourcing

On a similar topic, the changing global economy is causing businesses to change their procedures. While producing goods or supplying services may be too cost prohibitive in one country, another nation may be able to supply it much more cheaply. Where the one nation could focus on core competencies or doing what they do best, they can provide valuable work to the other country that is capable of executing the work more efficiently. Call centers, clothing manufacturers, petroleum workers, airplane manufacturers, and many others assemble products and provide services on an international scale. If you have such experience, you can guide a business to successfully outsource.

Organic Farming

So many people want to get back to the "good old days" where available food was fresher and contained fewer chemicals. Organic farming is a specialized industry made up of a growing number of supporters. Many want a healthier lifestyle, to save the planet, and improve their community's economic growth. Whatever the reason, this is a fantastic opportunity to lead with your experience. People know how to farm, but few can write and teach. Others want to learn about organic farming. Maybe that's where you can help.

Whole foods

Whole food stores are beginning to sprout. They offer fresh from the farm and unprocessed foods. They tend to have a small community and earthy feel to them. With a growing popularity, there is a need to provide information about introducing such a concept to those who are unfamiliar. Likewise, whole foods enthusiasts want to learn more. Do you have recipes, ideas for making farming or logistics to market easier, or a great idea on attracting customers? Can you make food stay fresh for longer periods?

Cleaning services

More and more families are moving into larger homes, earning dual incomes, or experiencing similar situations that leave little time for domestic chores. Homes, businesses, and non-profit organizations all need to be clean and safe. Cottage industries are springing up, but not fast enough to meet this growing need. This niche can be further specialized by the type of cleaning necessary. Animal and human waste, hazardous material, residence, professional and other sanitation needs create a continuous opportunity for experts to emerge and take charge.

Hazardous disposal

Poisonous, biological, chemical, medical, crime scene, and other waste must be disposed of properly. Federal and state laws, public opinion, and public relations all guide requirements for the safe and proper cleanup of hazardous material. Each type of disposal has its own unique requirements and may have its own professional organization, certification, and/or license requirement. Personal protective equipment may be part of the growing safety requirements. If you have the expertise to lead and teach the proper disposal of hazardous material, or help others get certified or licensed, there are great opportunities available for you to get started.

Homes

Today, families are busier and have unique needs. Single parent, dual income, multiple careers, and other family dynamics may make it difficult for some to keep their homes clean. Or, if they do have time to conduct simple cleaning, deep cleaning is just not possible. Children are as busy in sports, recreation, and volunteer opportunities. Do you have a product or service that can help? Do you know of a process for faster cleaning? Can you encourage or provide know-how to those in the cleaning industry? If so, this is a niche ready for help.

Auto detail

Consumers spend a lot of money on their vehicles. They are not just modes of transportation, but status symbols on which some may spend more than 50% of their annual income. Cars create an image that owners are willing to maintain at almost any expense. Other industries are growing to support this need. In my neighborhood, there are automated and hand wash stations to help get cars clean. There are also entrepreneurs who travel to residential or commercial locations to repair and detail automobiles. They are equipped with everything needed to keep a vehicle looking shiny and new. Professionals clean vents, carpets, windows, engines, trunks, wheel wells, and any other surface and interior area. The providers of such services also need their products maintained and stocked. If you have experience or a desire to provide excellent service, consider becoming such an expert and leading others to be better and more efficient auto detailers or cleaners.

Consulting

A consultant is a specialist who guides personnel and organizations to find solutions. Even an expert in a niche industry cannot know everything. For example, a human resource specialist may be familiar with insurance policies, hiring procedures, and workers compensation issues. However, the organization may be presented with challenges in leadership growth. An organization transitioning from a small, easy to manage organization to a large, fast growing enterprise may find change difficult. They find it hard to understand the training, documentation, certification, and legal issues necessary to meet growth requirements. The human resource specialist is an expert at small company affairs; however, she may contact a consultant who specializes in human resources management and professional growth. The consultant would not be hired to perform traditional tasks. They would be paid to help the company prepare to meet the challenges of managing growth.

Almost all industries have consultants. Consultants in general may not be considered a niche industry; the term is just too broad. But when providing advice and guidance in a particular discipline, they are then performing in a niche. Human resources, security, financial, pet grooming, program management, legal, quality control, finance, organization, and so on, are but a few of the possibilities. Perhaps you are a consultant or strive to become one. As an expert with the time and know-how, people will call you to solve their problems.

Consultants are in great demand and clients are willing to pay their salaries. Some work on site in an office provided by their client's organization, while others work on limited projects.

IDENTIFYING THE EXPERT

So, how do potential customers find you? They find you because you are writing, blogging, and posting on social media sites. As you get connected with other professionals, you can refer people to consultants who have an expertise in an area that you cannot advise in. They will, in turn, refer business to you.

All you really need is to have the confidence and courage to recognize yourself as the expert you are or will become. Try your favorite search engine and see how many types of consultants you can find. It just may inspire you.

PUBLISHING

Though the need for publications like books and magazines abounds, the market for many specialized areas is just too small for traditional publishers to touch. This may seem like an obstacle to traditional publishing, but for you, it's an opportunity. What would your world be like if you could be the sole-source provider of books to people in your industry, group, or organization?

Maybe you already have a book idea and it's been rejected by a few publishers. Maybe publishing house X sent a letter explaining how the book wasn't right for them. Well, just maybe it's not. But it doesn't mean it's not the right book for your audience. Traditional publishing is the wrong way to provide the right product. Let me explain.

By its very nature, a niche market is so condensed and too small for a publisher to risk working with it. If the market is too small, the publisher may lose money even if everyone affected buys the books. Traditional publisher business models depend on a buyer base willing to purchase tens of thousands of books. These publishers rely on prominent shelf space and hot topics to appeal to the largest customer bases. Small niches that just don't produce the desired results for the traditional publishers are excellent markets for niche publishing marketing.

For example, a traditional publisher pays nearly $20,000 to get a book to market. The book retails for $60. They would have to sell 334 books just to break even. If the niche market is small, that is a bad business model.

Now, consider your model. Print on demand has little up-front costs, leaving you able to publish the same book for as little as $120. That same book at the same price sold to the same amount of people will net you $17,000 profit. Quite refreshing and that is why Red Bike Publishing has been so successful.

Hopefully while reading this, your mouth is watering with realized potential and opportunity. By ignoring the market, the traditional publishers have opened up incredible opportunities. As an author and publisher, you have a few choices to make in determining how to get your information to the public who so badly needs it. You can convince the traditional publishers to take a chance if your market just happens to be large enough, or you can find or become a niche publisher.

Some major publishers, businesses, and large organizations seek out partnership ventures with small niche businesses. The niche businesses are the ones corporations outsource to. Outsourcing allows large enterprises to focus on their talents and abilities, while the niche groups provide products and services from their subject matter expertise. Working with niche organizations is a winning situation for the larger corporation, as well as the niche organization.

Publishing Opportunities Available in Specialized Industries

When it comes to writing and publishing, some niches are too small for large publishers to delve into. Efforts expended in small markets just don't provide the return on investment to cover overhead costs and make a profit. The customer footprint is too small to provide revenue and value. The overhead costs of writing, designing, editing, printing, and finding a target audience may far exceed the revenue provided by actual book sales. In many cases the needs of the niche are great, but the market just doesn't support all-out traditional publishing.

Traditional Publishing Opportunities

Remember my certification book? An editor I consulted on a niche idea told me the idea was too small. However, after recognizing a working potential, he later contacted me about another book idea directed to a more general security market. My niche book idea had led the way to a book deal with a traditional publishing company. The credentials I developed along the way to becoming a recognized expert in the profession and the proven market were enough for the editor to agree to publish a book. This is one of the potential benefits of working in a specialized industry.

Markets tend to cross. Think of the entertainment industry, where many singing groups are distinguished as crossover artists. They may specialize in rock or pop music, and come upon a hit that is recognized by the country market or vice versa. Being creative people in general, entrepreneurs also cross into other specialized markets. Some niches do apply to others rather easily.

Being Everywhere at Once

One of my colleagues asked me when I have time to sleep. I have given the impression that not only am I an expert at work, but also in my small business. He sees my book, press releases, posts on social networks, and articles in professional newsletters. Am I everywhere? Do I work day and night? Do I sleep? Am I super-human? Only to those who are standing on the outside.

You, on the other hand, will learn the secret to being omnipresent. You only need to make redundancy your best friend. Redundancy of marketing efforts will put you everywhere. Because of your redundant market efforts within your specialized industry, people will soon be commenting on finding your articles or comments online while searching for industry information on their favorite search engine.

Niche Expert Status

The key is an online presence so powerful that your website and books are the first ones listed on the search engine results page. Specializing in small categories allows you to do just that. While others spend tens of thousands of dollars for advertising, you can get better results. When someone searches a key word, they find you as the top choice for meeting their demands. Again, it doesn't cost money and you get to do what you like to do: write and promote yourself and your business.

Becoming Noticed at Work

Can your books get you noticed at work? My boss recently called me into his office.

"Shut the door," he said. "We need to have a quiet discussion." I quickly shut the door not knowing what to expect.

"Congratulations, you've been assigned the supervisor position you applied for. We reviewed your resume and out of all the candidates, you were best qualified. The leadership trait you excelled in was written communication, especially your impressive publications. Your resume and books really set you above the others."

No kidding. There I was getting kudos at work for the publishing company I ran at home.

Unfortunately, I hear too many comments from authors who claim not to be motivated by money or any other gain other than the pride of publishing. Personally, I find payment as a reward for good writing to be very motivating. I also find the prestige of being recognized by readers and invited to speak on niche topics rejuvenating. Why else do it?

Professional, personal and financial gains are great benefits of publishing. If you've got it, let everyone know. Marketing isn't a game for the timid.

Quitting your Day Job

The benefits of niche work continue to manifest in that your book just may allow you to quit that day job. It may just be big enough. My publishing mentor, William Henderson, wrote the book *Security Clearance Manual: How To Reduce The Time It Takes To Get Your Government Clearance.*

Talk about a niche market! He did something big and powerful. After spending more than two decades investigating people for security clearances, he put his experience on paper and wrote an amazing book. He also contributes articles to a major industry online magazine, allowing him to continue a significant presence. His self-published books are in libraries, college classrooms, and relied upon by many professionals in the security industry. Talk about an unexpected runaway hit. He controls his publishing destiny and keeps all the money. That's what specialized markets can do for you.

Those of you working in a niche market may already have a full-time job, and all of this writing and marketing is done while the rest of the world sleeps. If that's the case, you are not alone. Please don't let this hard work discourage your dreams of running your own business full time or someday being a self-supported author/publisher. As of this writing, I am working full time, managing a side niche business while trying to branch out into a more generalized field (publishing).

MY NICHE EXPERIENCE

My book on certification has a potential core market of over three thousand five hundred people belonging to the related professional organization. The market is expandable to the approximately twenty-five thousand people who are eligible for the certification, but are not part of the professional organization. As you may remember from the first chapter, I am very passionate about helping people pass this certification. The benefits to their career range from job security to promotion, even during difficult economic times.

After conducting in-depth target market research, I provided a marketing plan and a proposal to a traditional publishing company. About a week later, I received a call from an acquisitions representative. He said the book idea had merit, but the audience was just too small. Remember, the potential audience was up to fifteen thousand people, but it was not enough for the publisher to take the risk. That was when I decided to do some research and start my own publishing company that would allow me to provide training, resources, and products to the specialized industry.

To date, Red Bike Publishing has sold thousands of copies of *ISP and ISOC Master Exam Prep*. That may not seem like much, but keep in mind that small markets produce great returns. One thousand books multiplied by the $60 for every book sold on *Amazon.com* adds up to $60,000, a pretty decent return. You can get those results from your book in your specialized industry, not to mention the earnings from spin-off opportunities (I'll cover those later). We now have seven other titles and continue to grow.

Here is how we have made a difference. To date, there are a few thousand people certified; when I started, there were only one hundred fifty people. I was one of only four in my city, and those numbers are growing as well. My book is meeting an incredible need.

Now, a word of caution. As you become active in social networking, you may come across discussion groups that compare self-publishing with traditional publishing. Try not to get in the middle of the mudslinging and futile comparisons. All publishing methods are different. What I am proposing is becoming a self-publisher and using print-on-demand technology or eBooks to distribute your books. This is not a traditional publishing model and there is no way to compare the two. Both have their benefits and shortfalls. What we do as self-publishers for niche industries requires a different marketing and distribution effort and I do believe you can make more money self-publishing your book.

I can call my self-published books a success because sales have exceeded the demand for the certification, I have a positive number in my bank account, I outsource design and editing and I can increase my contributions to my favorite charities. My gift to the profession is spreading awareness of not only my book, but the certification. My job is to convince professionals not only to buy the book, but first to desire the certification. My potential includes the possibility of helping professionals grow in their careers. The benefit: earn a potential income of up to six hundred thousand dollars. Meeting demands with self-publishing for small niches doesn't sound so bad after all.

SUMMARY

Specialized markets are perfect opportunities to introduce products without having to borrow money or put down large amounts of cash. Because of the very nature of a niche, there are voids that you can fill. I've listed a few specialized markets and ways that an entrepreneur and author can establish themselves as an expert and provide valuable contributions. You make money almost immediately. Typical traditional publishing models cannot support the demands of small niches. However, niche and self-publishing models are perfect. You can tap into the markets where you are an expert and grow your business exponentially. Specialized markets are hurting for experts who are easily accessible and know how to communicate.

REVIEW QUESTIONS

1. Write a paragraph describing your niche.

2. What sub-niches can your idea be broken down into?

3. What information can you contribute to the sub-niches?

4. In what ways do you consider yourself an expert in those sub-niches?

CHAPTER 4   BECOME AN EXPERT

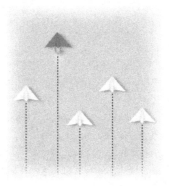

INTRODUCTION

To be able to write about a subject or serve an audience, you should be an expert. An expert should be able to communicate what they know and demonstrate their expertise. Those who actually have put into practice and experienced what they have learned are experts. The author who just regurgitates what they have read will not be able to offer much more than a synopsis or rewrite of a subject already covered. In a specialized industry, your audience is comprised of people hungry to learn how to be the best and they will easily recognize both the expert and the impostor.

ACCELERATING YOUR EXPERTISE TIMELINE

Several years ago, I made a phone call to another business to discuss a contract requirement. The person on the other end was hesitant to discuss the matter with me. She did not know who I was and seemed uncomfortable relaying any requested information. Consequently, I felt uncomfortable asking for the information I needed to get the job done.

I determined, then and there, that those within my profession would know my name within five years. I developed that plan and committed it to paper and even included it in Appendix A. Also, visit *www.redbikepublishing.com/nicheworkbook* for an electronic version.

Part I - Resources to Become an Expert

Learning is a part of the very important process of becoming an expert. Read all the publications, newsletters, blogs, and websites about your particular niche. Attend residence or online classes, webinars and seminars. Take all the education opportunities available within your specialized industry. Once you have the fundamentals down, then you can start to train others. Below is a wealth of information on places where you can learn and grow in a specialized area.

Expert Advice-Be sure to open an incognito window. This allows you to search for topics without your search results being tracked.

Newsletters

Newsletters are traditionally generated by professional organizations, hobbyists, and other groups for the reading pleasure and education of those with similar interests and motivations. Newsletters are a great way to learn more about a specialized area, as well as who the current experts are and what obstacles may need to be overcome. Use the newsletters and identified experts to conduct your market research.

Learn who is advertising, writing, or otherwise considered leaders in the industry. You can also use newsletters to discover gaps in education that you may be able to fill. If you have a hard time finding newsletters, try a Google search to find your specialized industry interest and their publications. You can program Google to perform a 24 hour 7 day a week search of groups, blogs and newsletters using niche related key words.

Blogs

Blogs are similar to newsletters, but often less formal. Many professions and organizations use blogs to reach their members. Blogs help increase awareness as most are public and keyword searchable. You can learn about the latest industry trends, read comments and feedback provided by customers and audience members. You can find specialized blogs through keywords on your favorite search engine.

Websites

Many professionals have a website that can be used to perform in-depth research into your chosen niche. However, don't just limit your searches to professional organizations. Hobbies, enthusiasts and clubs also provide great avenues for blogs, newsletters and other publications. You would also do well to research suppliers, vendors, and consultants within the industry. Such research will give you a good handle on products and services offered as well as what is lacking. The research may also provide you with fresh ideas for products and services that your unique skill sets meet. Also, lack of search results may indicate critical information gaps that you can fill.

Online classes

Many organizations offer free and inexpensive training. Consider the free stuff first. Companies offer training as a way to gather mailing list information and other data. White papers and PowerPoint presentations may be the only resources available. That could be a bonus for you since your upcoming book could address the lack of response and provide just what the market needs.

Residence classes

Colleges, adult education, churches, non-profit organizations, and professional groups all offer low-cost and free seminars and classes. Usually they bring in the experts and attract the best students. These are great places to network and get your name out there at the same time.

Webinars

Webinars are web seminars and are similar to online and residence classes. Video and other inexpensive software help reduce costs and allow affordable production. Webinars are almost just as good as being there in person. Students can interact with each other and the presenters.

Social Networking Activities

Let me begin by saying that I no longer market heavily through social media. I found that in my niche, my customers used social media for the social aspect, but typically do not respond to ads, sign up forms or sales pitches. Most marketing books will encourage that activity, but I don't recommend it unless you want to be a social media influencer or your products are social media specific.

Otherwise, social media platforms such as LinkedIn, Twitter, Facebook and other emerging social networks are great online places to look for experts in your field. Many have started unique groups and other venues providing opportunities to meet others and learn from their experiences. You can also contribute while you learn in an informal university experience. The key is to build connections with those you know, as well as their contacts who may be involved in your niche. The more people you connect with, the better your message gets out and the more you can learn. Social networking sites can help you market your own book and discover niche ideas, as well as those broader interests related to your niche. You just might identify greater customer needs.

LinkedIn

LinkedIn is a network of professionals that has interactive groups, and most are easy to join. You will have the opportunity to put your current and past employment, education, recommendations, summary of you and your product, and many other applications.

Your input creates keywords that would link to profiles of other people who have listed similar information. Your job title, location, professional organization, company name, education, and other details will become links to similar profiles. This helps you, the niche marketer, to find others in your group or profession. For example, if your specialty is "technical writing for rebuilding steam powered antique trucks", key words would link to others who are involved in technical writing, rebuilding trucks, steam power, and antique trucks. You can gain an opportunity to discover groups and individuals with like skills and similar interests.

LinkedIn also has group and member updates that provide the latest information for your niche. I belong to writing, publishing, security, and government groups which express both my professional and personal interests. LinkedIn allows you to search groups by keyword or group name. Chances are that a specialized group may exist and, if not, you can create your own. Group membership allows you to read and respond to posts, create job announcements, and read industry or group related news.

Facebook

With Facebook as a social media alternative, the emphasis is on social. This is more relationship and brand building and may be the perfect opportunity to just discuss and encourage. Discussions and activities may or may not be as intense or focused as other social networks. However, you can still find experts in the field. Facebook allows businesses and organizations to build pages, communities, and groups, post messages, and link blogs and articles. It also keeps fans and group members up to date.

Some businesses have found out ways to make money using Facebook, selling products. Others have created private pages or groups for their members to interact and learn.

Twitter

Twitter is also easy to join. Once you create a profile, you can look up other people or organizations that you have an interest in and follow them to get their Tweets. You can create automatic links to tweet from online articles. You can use Twitter to identify experts, expand your networking, and learn as you read article links and connect with existing experts and follow links to their websites.

Caution: Social networking is a focused activity, but keep focused. You might be tempted to bring as many contacts as possible. But if they aren't niche related, they will be a distraction.

Online Articles

Web magazine sites such as *About.com, eHow.com* and *ezinearticles. com* have contributions by many experts writing on various topics. I've learned publishing tips, researched security article ideas, learned to write better, and much more. Not only can you read informative articles, but you can get information about the authors by viewing their profiles. The beauty is that you don't need a membership to do this research. However, the benefits of becoming a member are tremendous.

You can search these magazines for articles related to your specialized area and have alerts sent to your email account concerning articles that fit your interests. Though you won't be able to get notifications in niche specific areas, you can select articles appealing to a broad interest such as business, writing, home improvement, and many other major subcategories.

Now that you've learned, get noticed as an expert

As you learn and grow in the industry, you can begin to make your mark. Even if all you are doing is posting information about all of the training and education you are involved in on your social networks, blogs, website, and networking locations, you are getting a message out. Tweets such as: "___ is learning how to use magnifying glasses to help assemble model train villages" will attract hobbyists to your Twitter profile. Or for safety conscious industries, post about how much you enjoyed ladder safety classes to help attract others.

Volunteer to lead a discussion, group, committee or other problem solving body

A business owner friend of mine is doing incredible work for the government. She provides a great product and is spearheading a service that is going to create great revenue for her company. Additionally, she'll be able to hire more employees as the opportunities start to open. This work came after a struggle with how people viewed the company's capabilities. Though focused primarily in the commercial industries, she had tremendous experience working on government contracts and technology.

Undaunted, she joined a related professional organization and quickly chaired a committee with some of the industry's leading influencers. It was this volunteer work that earned her well-deserved credibility and opened doors for her company's current success.

If you are already a well-established expert, then begin to expand your notoriety with various online tools. Take time to write, teach, and attract an audience online and in person. Begin creating your own publications. Create newsletters, post original blog material, and improve your website to reflect your strengths as an expert in the specialized market. You can assemble online classes and webinars, or create seminars. Continue to learn, but begin to teach at all opportunities available within your specialization. When you have the fundamentals down, you can start to train others.

Part II - Same Resources to Demonstrate Expertise

You've studied, attended presentations, sought expert opinion, and practiced your skills; now show them what you've got. The best way to do that is to help fellow professionals, offer products, and inform them. As you provide information, you can market your books, products, and business. Informative articles paired with points of sale will propel your business. The methods I recommend are to provide small articles for blogs, websites, newsletters, social networks, and everything else listed below. Then, liberally apply links to where your books and products are sold.

When demonstrating yourself as an expert, always have a call to action or point of sale. I like to leave points of contact, a link to my website page for a free download, a way to subscribe to my newsletters, a link to purchase books, and so much more. I want a way to invite the reader into a relationship.

Take the opportunity to invite the reader to respond as I have. Notice that in the beginning and the end of this book, I provided an invitation to download a gift and invited you to review this book. I'd be really happy if you took me up on those invitations. Whatever you do, let the audience know how they can respond, help, or join.

Blogs

Blogs are, by far, one of the best ways to demonstrate your knowledge. If you've become an expert show the world you know your subject by writing blog posts. Starting out is slow, but when you begin to accumulate articles, an amazing thing happens. People begin to recognize your writing, comment on your writing, and invite you to write and speak for them. Blog posts are also great subject matter for future books. So, write, write and write. The more posts, the more opportunities to get noticed.

My blogs are the number one marketing method for Red Bike Publishing. Each of my books has a blog, as well as my publishing company. As my subject matter became better known, amazing things happened for my company. As industry related businesses are advertising, I am invited to guest blog and editors actually contact me for articles. I haven't sent a query letter out in years. Now, I have supplemental income and marketing through a standing invitation to write for a security magazine.

Your blog helps you connect with your customer, and deliver a high level of commitment as regular input is needed. Think of a blog as a diary or journal type of entry. Higher frequencies of shorter articles are better, so save the longer messages for newsletters and your book. For simplicity and efficiency, my newsletters, blogs, and books have similar content and material. You can get your own blog by setting up an account with *www.blogspot.com, www.wordpress.com* or any other provider that fits your needs.

When you start your blog, be sure to include as much information about your business as you can in your profile. Fill out your profile information completely and use good keywords to direct traffic to your blog. Upload pictures of you and your products. If you have a book published, make sure you have a link to *Amazon.com* and your website where the books can be purchased. Don't forget to offer free information and have a sign-up for your newsletter.

Use your blog to direct visitors to your website, make purchases, join your newsletter, and learn more about you and your business. Be keyword rich in your posts so search engines can find them. For example, if your niche is janitorial services and you sell environmentally safe cleaning detergent, you might provide a link from the keyword detergent to your website product. In other words, if your post is about the best detergent to use to clean up grease, link the word "detergent" to your website. You might link the work " janitor" or "clean" to the book information page on your website.

If you don't have enough material to start your own blog, or you are not committed to a blog, you can comment on other related blogs. When you post comments on other blogs, you can link your website to your comment. When others read your comments, they can instantly find your website. Take an interest in the topic you comment on. People can tell if you are marketing, so make your comments genuine.

Newsletters

An excellent way to gain credibility is to start your own newsletter. If you've started your blog, then turn your posts into articles. Blogging and newsletter updating provides great writing, editing, and marketing practice. Regular input exercises your creativity, and the research you do is invaluable in helping you build your knowledge.

When your audience reads your newsletters and forwards issues to colleagues, this demonstrates a clear marketing success in itself. Your audience will find your content helpful and useful, and will forward them. They will ask permission to republish articles in their organization's newsletters and much more. The contact information and website addresses within the newsletter content lead others to you and the outreach opportunities continue to grow. Soon, your newsletter activity will cause you to be recognized as an expert in your field.

Newsletter formatting can be as simple as using a word document or email. You can also use more complicated software or join a professional newsletter website. The most important thing about newsletters is getting the right message to the right people. If you provide a newsletter but don't have a relevant audience, then it won't be effective. A good way to get a newsletter going is to contribute articles to another existing and more prominent newsletter. Pretty soon, people will be able to recognize your name and assume you are an industry leader.

I recommend using a newsletter service that will manage subscriptions for you. You will want to be able to capture new subscribers, create subscriber lists, target those lists with specific messages, and keep them updated with news and products.

The service should provide newsletter templates. Most importantly, they should offer a way for potential customers to sign up for your newsletter and verify the subscription. As soon as the person signs up for your newsletter, they will automatically begin receiving it. The beauty is this service will provide a way for you to program as many messages as you want, at any time you command.

For example, my website has a place for people to subscribe to my newsletter. Once they join, they receive a few scheduled newsletters and each month, I write a fresh edition. Additionally, since my book is about a certification, I also send out sample certification review questions every few weeks. Every few months, my scheduled product catalogue goes out as well. The entire process from customer subscription, receiving the newsletter and removal requests is automated. IContact is the service that I use and manages my newsletters and emails and puts controls in place so that I don't accidentally SPAM my audience.

Your newsletter also has other possibilities. I recommend that you begin with a catchy title tied to your subject. This should include keywords that will help people find you using their search engine. If you are using a service to handle your newsletter distribution, they may offer a way to archive your newsletter for future reading. When archived, others will be able to find your work on the Internet through pre-established keywords.

Always refer people back to your website. The contact information also gives the impression of a professional publication. Speaking of professional, go ahead and add a publication or issue number. A great header and logo will lend credibility and help brand your newsletter with your business.

Begin your publication with your articles. You can copy and paste from your blogs or vice versa. Use keywords relative to the industry in your articles. Also, add links that will bring readers to your book information. If you copy and paste from your blog, the hyperlinks you may have already added will transfer to the newsletter.

Provide three or four 500-600 word articles. They shouldn't be too long as it may cause the readers to lose interest. Keep them short and to the point, and use plenty of stories, real life examples, and anecdotes. People relate well to articles that explain a situation and offer solutions.

It's even better when you can put articles in story form. The nice thing about these shorter articles is that they may be used word for word in a blog or other postings. You will have to determine whether or not the mood or style of the article suits blog material. If so, use it word for word. If not, change it up a bit.

List solutions in the article title. If your article is about writing books, then the title might be "Five Easy Methods to Prevent Writer's Block." Then use five bullet comments that solve the problem up front, then expand the bullets with relevant anecdotes.

After your articles, add information about your company, other books, and related events. This is an important piece of your marketing. Welcome your readers in each issue, thank your new subscribers, and recommend that all readers forward the newsletter.

The "From the Editor" column should also mention any news you might have concerning your business. Are you signing books, providing training, or reaching important milestones? Great news should be shared with your audience. Include any training you've attended or certification you've earned. Basically, this is the most important real estate on your newsletter. Use it to attract interest, drive more traffic to your website, and let everyone know other places you are effective.

You can also accept advertisements in your newsletter. I've saved a place in my newsletter for business sponsors. Not everyone will want to sponsor your newsletter, so give them a good reason to do so. I like to give sponsors space on my newsletter, websites, and blogs all for one low price. The businesses I contact operate in the same specialized area that I do. When I contact prospective sponsors, I let them know that, even though my customer base is small, it is made exclusively of their desired customer base. All are qualified buyers. In other words, the audience is niche specific. The message goes directly to those they are trying to reach. Not a bad risk on the sponsor's part.

If you'd like to join my self-publishing newsletter, please email me @ editor@redbikepublishing.com.

Podcast

A podcast is a great way to engage your customers and attract new people to your business. I have two podcasts called _DoD Secure_ and _Book Based Business Incubator_. I invite guests who are experts in both topics to speak and share experiences. Other times, I do a monologue to talk about security clearance issues or publishing and book business topics. It's a great way to expose more people to my books and services. Podcasts are easy to set up. In the beginning I just used my phone and some recording software. You just need a way to capture the conversation, edit it, and submit it. I use a service called Buzzsprout and they are great.

Website

Websites are another solution allowing niche marketers to become INTERNET superstars. Niche publishing and topics make it possible for you to get your book to your customers through online bookstores such as Amazon, Barnes and Noble, and many more. It's no longer necessary to be published by a major company to get your message out. Now, you can publish hardcover and paperback books for less than $150 per title. You earn revenue with very little risk. Even if your title sells no books, you risk only the setup fees. You can also write and sell eBooks with no costs or setup fees.

For example, an author can publish their works, sell them with little overhead, and make the books available on the Internet. Instead of receiving eight to fifteen percent of sales with publishing houses, authors can now write a book, sell it online and pocket all the profit. This has never existed before.

Here are some great pros for self-publishing.

- No fees or startup costs
- Inexpensive marketing possibilities
  - Write articles in newsgroups and ezines
  - Blog regularly
  - Review books on *Amazon.com* and other areas (use name and website in profile)
  - Email campaigns
- Web pages are inexpensive
- No need to buy or rent property

The Internet offers great opportunities to start a business with minimal startup costs. Some successful authors who sell books online and practice online affiliations earn income from ingenious methods. As technology progresses, we will see new types of business springing up. Keeping this in mind, an attractive and informative website is crucial, but huge expenses are not. You want to attract potential customers, allow them to connect with you quickly, view products, and develop enough trust to buy products.

Websites should offer at least a few fundamental pieces of information. Surf the net and find winning websites that demonstrate professionalism and allure that a customer just can't resist. When designing your website, take advantage of the space available to inform customers of what you have and draw them into making a buying decision.

About Us

Everyone wants to know what makes you the expert; tell them. List your certifications, education, and affiliations with professional organizations, universities, and other businesses. It helps the customer connect your product with experience.

Contact

How do customers and potential customers contact you? Websites look more professional when contact information is listed. A word of warning: some people may abuse the contact information, so make sure you provide an address or phone number that isn't for primary home use.

Sign up form

Be sure to have a sign up form to allow people to join your newsletter or mailing list. You should be able to generate these forms using the email marketing or service provider.

Products or Services

Tell about your product and/or services and why someone should buy it. This page is used to make an emotional connection with the customer that causes them to make a purchase. What will the product do for the customer? Why should the customer spend the money and time on your product? We don't want a list of product offerings, but a connection with how the product can help us. Consider using a page for each of the products. Then, link your products with a point of sale. Will you use PayPal or direct customers to *Amazon.com*? Make choices easy and obvious for customers.

References, Recommendations or Testimonials

As you begin to make sales, ask for comments from your customers that you can post on your website or blog, *Amazon.com*, and other places. Obviously, only list those positive comments that help you sell more products. Be sure to ask for full names, titles, and locations.

Links to Blogs or Podcasts

If you have a blog or podcast, make sure to integrate it with your website. Every time you blog, it will appear on your page as new and relevant information. This keeps your website fresh and up to date.

Other information

Of course, this list is not all that is possible to put on a website. Be sure to include reasons to get people to enter contests, join newsletters, or give feedback. Creative ways of making sales or getting permission to include contact information for your mailing list is essential.

 Also, offer something for free. You can offer books, newsletters, promotional products, eBooks, etc. Give away Internet based products or products that you can forward from Internet orders. Mailing and packaging is expensive and time consuming. Free items tend to get passed around within friend and peer groups. This increases awareness of you and your products. Free stuff also brings people back to your website. I have offered a free slide show that complements my certification book. While the book focuses on technical data, the slide show instructs methods for successfully taking online exams.

Online classes

What I love about my specialized market is that customers are hungry for knowledge. Many seek me out because of the articles I've written and the local training I give. My newsletters, blogs, website, and social networking posts all point to the different methods I use for helping others understand our industry. For example, when I teach my classes at night school, I post the topic to my blog.

For the sake of clarification, I will refer to online classes as information that you provide for customers to download or subscribe to. I use both methods. These are not generally live, interactive events, but just great downloadable information. Online classes can be presentations with a script read by a narrator or simply something the student will read or lead on their own.

I have used website development tools to create my own classes at BennettInstitute.com. I used my book material to develop classes and create content. I record my classes using Zoom, upload them to video hosting site like Vimeo and assemble into classes on my website. In fact, one of the appealing and common features is the ability to use PowerPoint presentations and make videos of myself presenting the information.

I also offer PowerPoint presentations of required security training. In my niche, there is a requirement for employees to take mandatory training. Organizations are inspected on whether or not the training is conducted. People who are new to the business desire education material that they can use to formulate their training.

I like to provide training in three methods. The first is training that my audience can download and brief to their clients. The script is already written and I give them the option of tailoring the script to meet their needs. The second option is to provide the presentations for their clients to study on their own. This self paced training still meets the requirements and frees my customer's time. Again, these reflect the work I've already created in my writings. The third method is to provide the training in email form. I send the presentation to the customer and they broadcast it through their email. This presentation cannot be tailored or altered. It is designed to provide a quiz, print a certificate, and notify my customer that the training was conducted.

Going back to my passion to teach security professionals how to study for the security certification, I am happy to offer a course in exam preparation. I give students an idea of how the test is conducted and how they can focus their study time to pass the test. The great thing with the certification is that it is based on an open book exam. The certification owner requires that students meet certain prerequisites. Certification candidates must have worked in the industry for five years and should perform at least 10% of their work time on the test topic. This is important because I can design a test preparation training that I know only experts will take. Absolute beginners are disqualified from taking the exam.

What does that mean to me? I can design a study aid that helps build my customers' confidence. I am not teaching them something that they don't know, I'm just reinforcing their knowledge. I do this by showing them how to find answers in the resources available to them. The test is challenging, however I build their confidence and make them more apt to take the exam. I've helped many get certified who may have not otherwise taken the exam.

Additionally, I started a new website called BennettInstitute.com. I've recorded classes for both the security and book based business niches. I get to provide best-selling training that helps students get ahead in their security careers. I also teach authors and publishers about starting book based businesses. I notify my newsletter subscribers when I launch new training. Visit BennettInstitute.com to see an example of courses.

Webinar

If you decide to run a webinar, make sure it is fun and informative. Remember, this is where you will interact with a group of students. You can use information that you've written in books, articles, or other publications to create a learning experience for others. A webinar can be created using any one of the topics you used to create an online or downloadable training class. For example, I might create a webinar on the topic of how to take the certification test. I could use already available information and walk a live audience through the test taking process. Theoretically, I could have hundreds of people in the webinar as opposed to just a few at a residence course.

Residence classes

This is a real opportunity to build credentials and create a real academic presence. Traditional education opportunities are solid and recognized ways to get your message out and establish you as the expert. Teaching provides a return on investment, but takes hard work and persistence to get started. Also, there are two different avenues: you can host these classes yourself, or you can get them sponsored.

Host the Residence Class Yourself

Just like self-publishing, you can control the product. You have the freedom to create and do not need to seek approval from anyone to get started. You choose to set up the class time, the material, the advertising, and everything else you need to start a successful course. It also means that you have to bring in the resources yourself. For a residence class, you will need a classroom or similar environment, curriculum, projector, screen, training aids, certificates, and supplies. There is a terrific possibility for high overhead costs. Unless you already have the means, you may need to rent space.

You will also need to be prepared to conduct a lot of administrative tasks. These include advertisement, registration, payment, copies, course material, setting up contracts for rooms, agreements with students, and creating a compelling reason for students to come to you. This will require a significant amount of organization, discipline, and follow through.

Organization/Business/University Hosted

This is a great way to gain instant credibility, earn an income, and teach without having to worry about the administrative tasks. When sponsored, the space, advertising, registration, payment, and graduation certificate requirements are already taken care of. You can also negotiate a good salary. I used to teach a security course using my security books for required reading. That adds up to a nice paycheck. The process is already institutionalized and all you have to do is show up, sort of.

One of the great benefits of being a niche publisher/author is your customers' recognition of you as the subject matter expert. This leads to more book sales, teaching and speaking opportunities. I taught security courses at the University of Alabama in Huntsville. The following describes how I planned for and got the job of teaching at university and professional organization hosted venues.

I started with a proposal and will show you the method I have taught to several colleagues. It is designed to help convince an organization to hire you to teach in your area of expertise. If you apply it well, it only serves to enforce that you are a subject matter expert, you've done the necessary research, there is a viable market, and they want to see you teach it.

Think of this from the sponsoring organization's point of view. They need to answer the tough questions to provide funding and resources for your presentations.

1. Who will take this course? Sponsors want to know how to reach their target audience. You've already done the market research, now you can demonstrate to them who the audience is and how to reach them.

2. How many potential students will sign up? This is a tough question, but you can demonstrate an audience response through book sales, how many people are in your newsletter, how many people read blogs you contribute to, and other statistics.

3. What are the students willing to pay? This is a little easier to find with some basic research. What are others paying for the same information at similar venues?

4. Why should they take the course? Demonstrate how students need continuous learning credits, how they will get a unique edge, the new skill they will learn, how the training meets a requirement, etcetera.

5. Will we recover our expenses and make a profit? This is an important question from the sponsor's point of view. You can help them determine the return on investment by working out your salary, how much you will do to help advertise (tons), how many students you need for the course to be a "go", and what materials each party is required to present.

It's up to you to provide those answers. Don't leave the marketing questions for them to figure out. Once you do the work and have a successful presentation, you can do much more with less investment. In my case, I've presented many times in the same venue. The university realized a profit and invited me back regularly. You can do the same. Oh yes, once successful, be sure to put that in your blog, website, and social network pages.

Because it is resource heavy, you will need a good pitch to get it going. When you contact a potential sponsor, ensure them that you are the expert in the reported topic by introducing yourself as such. Prior to contacting the University of Alabama in Huntsville, I had already established myself as an expert. My articles, blog, and social network posts had paved the way. The education and training I attended also gave credibility to my efforts. In fact, I used those experiences to produce a precise and concise proposal to the university's decision maker.

Due to the nature of specialized markets, there may not be a publication, instruction, or criteria already in place. I ƒnot only had to create the criteria, but develop a comprehensible study of the potential student population. This was already available and may be available to you by following the process recommended in this book. As I built my platform, I had made a connection with my customers. Also, I understand the industry and the type of education they craved. Now, students purchase my publishing company's books as required course material.

When writing your proposal, start with the title page. Put your title at the top and your contact information including address, phone number, and email address at the bottom. Next comes the meat of your work. Set your page to double-space and assign an appropriate font. I choose to use Times New Roman font size twelve. Your proposal should contain all the necessary information that we will cover below. Depending on your experience and the type of course you propose, your paper may be lengthy; mine is sixteen pages.

Begin with a summary statement of what you intend to accomplish with your training. This part is titled *A Synopsis of The Course.* Use this section to create interest and establish the need for your course, who it applies to, and why it is appropriate. For my security course, I constructed a compelling story of the need for an increase in the hiring of competent security managers. I also explained the required training and need for security managers to not only have technical competency, but to be able to understand the company's business. Without this training, security managers would not have a firm grasp of their role and value.

The next section is called *Goals.* Start with the bottom line up front, listing what you hope to accomplish. I demonstrated how security managers could exceed requirements while helping their companies stay within budget. I also conveyed that the training could help the security managers remain competitive for special awards available to those who passed inspections.

Next, create a new section called *Learning Objectives.* I listed the headings of my proposed lessons in bullet form as follows in the short sample:

- Becoming familiar with requirements
- Prioritizing protection efforts

- Security organizational structure
- Providing effective security training

The next section is *The Target Audience.* This is where marketing comes in. Since you are already looking into expressing yourself as an expert, you've probably already built up a platform or at least have an understanding of those who may want to take your training. Be specific here.

I listed the number of potential students, companies they worked for, and the need for training of those in the immediate area. This section will strengthen your position with the sponsoring organization. It gives them a reason to risk the resources they will pour into your presentation.

The next section is *Special Market Opportunities.* If there are local professional organizations, clubs, seminars, certifications, or other ways to co-sponsor the training, list them here. I included the need for security professionals to prepare for certification, listed the professional organizations that could provide a means of free advertising, and the blogs and newsletters that I supported. If you have a built-in mailing list for newsletters or other opportunities or relationships to help get the word out, it can only strengthen your case. In one course I taught, I was able to get a professional organization to share expenses with the university. This linked me professionally with the university and the professional organization, which increased my marketing footprint and provided more members for my newsletters and mailing lists.

The next section is the *Class Syllabus.* If you are suggesting a new course, then you will most likely have to develop your own material. I developed my security course based on my manuscript a publisher was evaluating. I used the proposal to strengthen the applicability of the book as a text for the course. This is a synergy of how the book supports the course and the course supports the book. If you are walking into a course already developed, your purpose is to provide justification for why you are the right person to teach it.

I began with a description of each class that I listed in the *Primary Learning Objectives* section. I used bullet format to demonstrate a concise lesson by lesson description to support a course with 24 hours worth of material. You will have to determine the course length. Your responsibility is to justify the course and win full sponsorship. Your course may be longer or shorter depending on the need. If you have a book or are preparing one for publication, consider using chapter headings and bullet type descriptions as the curricula.

The next part is your credentials. Begin this section on a new page with the heading Curriculum Vitae. Your name and contact number should be on the next line on the left side of the page.

The next line entry will be very similar to a resume. Enter a few lines down and begin a *Professional Skills* section. Here, I listed my position and job titles expanding my career. It is just a long paragraph of job titles separated by commas. If you don't have a long list of titles, then list those that you have in bullet form.

The next section is *Education.* Under the word education, list the high schools and colleges if you've graduated. If you are still a student, list the schools and write that you are still attending. Education should be listed as Degree, Name of School, City and State, Grade Point Average (if 3.9 or 4.0).

Under traditional education, begin a section for Honors. This is where you list military, trade school, and other types of training institutions. You can list certifications, awards, and other special honors. Don't be shy; this is part of demonstrating your expertise in a specialized area.

Next is the *Employment and Experience section.* This is a chronological listing and description of your work experiences. Make sure that the work matches the course you intend to teach. If not, then find some transferable experience. A transferable experience is an unrelated skill that can be applied to the course. For example, leadership, initiative, administrative and speaking skills aren't exactly needed for dog groomers. However, they will strengthen your position as a trusted teacher or presenter of dog grooming topics.

Finally, list all of your publications. I like to list books, magazines, newspapers, newsletters, blogs, and other publications where my work has been published. You can even list your own publications that you have created. List them chronologically and use an approved publication method such as American Psychological Association (APA), Modern Language Association (MLA) or Chicago Style.

Summary

Becoming an expert and being recognized as an expert is a journey. While studying to become an expert, you can actually begin posting what you learn or publish your thoughts and impressions on the subject. Establish the background that makes you an expert later. You can do this while attending training, seminars, or just providing a review of books in your newsletters, blog posts, or on *Amazon.com*. Build your credentials as you learn. And whatever you do, don't stop learning or teaching. Then establish yourself as an expert by helping others.

Review Questions

1. Research blogs that relate to your niche interest. Bookmark the blogs for future reference.

2. Is there any specific niche-related material the blogs do not cover that you understand very well?

3. Which blogs will allow you to contribute as a guest blogger?

4. Are there voids in the niche area that you could cover in a blog of your own?

5. If you have developed an idea for a course (online, in person, or webinar) write it here.

6. Outline your idea with main topic and supporting topics.

7. Continue to develop these blogs and course material blogs until you can build a case for presenting.

CHAPTER 5 WRITE YOUR BOOK

INTRODUCTION

Putting a good solution in a printed or eBook is an increasingly valuable method of getting information to your audience. You can teach more people through a book distribution than you can in a limited classroom environment. It is also a great way to earn money. This chapter will demonstrate how to discover attractive book topics in your niche; the importance of budgeting your time; how to organize your thoughts into sections, chapters, and books; how to format your manuscript; and how to become recognized as an expert as you create your book.

WRITING YOUR BOOK

What goes on paper is a result of tireless effort. Depending on your motivation and personality, it may seem easier to put together a course or write an article or two for a newsletter, blog, or other publication. My intent for the earlier chapters of this book was to help you learn all you can about your specialized market and establish yourself as a niche expert. Writing is part of that process and writing a book length manuscript is difficult. It takes time, commitment, and some solitude, much of which a full-time professional does not have to begin with. However, combining blogs, newsletters, training, and other efforts reduces your workload.

The difficulty of formatting a book may not be as tough as setting aside time and committing to writing words on paper. For example, you might remember a show called ECO Challenge. The show featured well-groomed teams of athletes competing in exotic worldwide locations for the chance to be the best. Days of running, bike riding, canoing, swimming and many more events challenged the fittest. The winner wasn't always the fastest or the strongest. Champions, on most occasions, had a mindset that the race was long and each step counted. This attitude led a team of Playboy Playmates to beat groups of men trained by elite military units. The strategy of one step at a time led them to victory.

The endurance athlete is committed to the task of running many miles. They begin knowing they have a long distance to run. Similarly, as an author/publisher, you have already identified niches that aren't supplied by publications. The market is hungry for knowledge, but to date, none has been supplied. On the other hand, there might be many books published, but they don't completely meet the need. As an author, you are not necessarily writing to beat others to market, but to get a champion product that fulfills a need. It also may be a good assumption that, as you write, you will remain the sole source expert on the topic. Until you succeed, others may not even have the energy or desire to write about your subject area. Once you succeed, others may join you in the market.

Remember, your niche could be too small for publishers to venture into. Even if all the customers bought books, there wouldn't be enough sales to warrant the huge financial, time, and resource commitment required of a traditional publisher. This is a great opportunity because your market is protected. You have a built-in audience with no competition. All you have to do is commit to the project, organize your thoughts, complete a manuscript, edit the manuscript, and publish it.

I'll demonstrate two methods of publishing your efforts and making big sales. None of these suggestions involves getting your book in bookstores, signing with major publishing companies, or a success model involving a lot of wasted effort trying to replicate traditional publishing or traditional marketing efforts. The premise: you are writing for a niche, you've already found your audience.

Getting Started

A familiar saying, "Necessity is the Mother of Invention," describes that a need comes before a product. Someone recognized the absence of a product and met the need with their own invention. Many become wealthy and famous providing what they themselves found the world to lack.

In my case, it was the help I provided other professionals with practice tests and boosting their confidence to take a security certification. Before I took my certification exam, I looked around for leadership. There was none, and I found it was up to me to study for and pass the examination. So, I began to develop my own study program.

The ideas I developed were not conventional in the specialized security market. However, I had learned from college, and prior military and life experience, how to set goals and establish a way to reach those goals. I went about touching, experiencing, and researching everything I could about the certification. I volunteered for extra jobs at work (related to the certification) and took notes of my progress.

I also read reviews of the test and articles about who passed and how they studied. Most who had failed had done so because they ran out of time. Since the certification exam has a two hour time limit for 110 questions, I knew that my priority was to find the answers quickly.

When the day came, I took the test and finished in plenty of time. I realized that I held a key to passing the test and knew that I could share it with others. While others ran out of time, I found a way to beat the clock. My premise is that the professionals already know the material, and I can show them how to organize studying to successfully pass the test.

And that's the point. There was a problem and I knew I had the solution. Others continue to write to me, as well as post positive comments about my book. To date, I still have no serious competition, but others are arriving to the market. I just have to stay on top. My publications allow professionals to focus on their careers, knowing I will provide quality niche-related publications.

So, how can you help others? Do you have an idea inside just waiting to get out? Many successful products have come from developers and entrepreneurs who have stumbled onto a great way to help.

Addressing the problem

You may have already discovered a void or other problem in our niche market that you can fix. Hopefully, you've already established yourself as the expert as described in our first few chapters. If so, then you already have material for your book. If you've started an online or residence course, blog, podcast or newsletter, then that information can be turned into a book. Maybe it can even become the textbook for what you teach. If that's the case, you already have a customer base made up of past, present, and future students. If you already have a book, then you can begin to build a platform and slowly build trust within your market.

My book about certification has been in print since 2008, and *How to Get US Government Contracts and Classified Work* since 2011. Both are continuing to sell well. Why? Because they are still relevant, timely, people are talking and writing about them, and trusting the author and publishing company. This sends two messages. First, the audience will discover you. Second, the niche creates an opportunity to publish a book topic that may not go out of date.

You might be capable of writing a book whether or not anyone knows about you. While building your platform, you can gain credibility as a subject matter expert. Soon, people will be contacting you to speak and write. A book can propel you from obscurity to an expert sought after for interviews and quotes. Why? Because your book answers a need.

In niche markets, there are many opportunities for writers to address and assist. If information is limited, you can help with informative book after book. You may also have opportunities for spin-off products. When you meet one need, you can continue with the next, and have a following of dedicated customers.

One opportunity you might discover is the lack of published information. That's where you come in. The best way to get there may be to compile all of your articles and blogs. If you've been maintaining a blog and newsletter, you may already have a following of readers eagerly anticipating your updates. These make up your potential book buyers. They may appreciate an expert opinion or teachings concerning their particular specialized industry. People are hungry for knowledge and are willing to pay for it. They always buy good books that help them improve their position, knowledge, education, and careers. Self-improvement and professional books make up a large publishing demand. It's up to you to know what your audience craves and how to provide it.

Book Content and Format

The format of the book is very much up to you. You should follow a successful formula based on similar successful books. You may notice that books are in different formats based on the publisher and the type of book. As long as your book looks professional and gives the desired information in an easy to understand method, it will meet your customer's needs.

I like the format used in many modern non-fiction "how to" books. The paragraphs look blocked, there is plenty of white space and lots and lots of paragraph and page headers. This format keeps me better focused and organized both as a reader and author. Many chapters have sub-chapters using this format. You can see this format throughout this book. I use Microsoft Word to format my manuscript with justified paragraphs. They are not centered, left or right. They are crisp and have straight lines throughout. Once complete, I build my final manuscript using Adobe InDesign.

My other books have been published in a more traditional approach. I've aligned the text to the left side, indented the beginning of paragraphs and begun new paragraphs on the next line. This is the format you might find in novels, term papers, and etc. This is widely accepted, but no longer my favorite method. However, if your professional taste prefers it, go for it.

The next part is breaking down the book into the proper format. Take a look at books on your bookshelf; each probably has a different format. If you self-publish, you should choose what fits your niche best. Find a book closely related to your subject and format it in a similar manner.

Planning Chapters

Most books have a table of contents. Usually a table of contents is developed after the book is written. However, I employ a different technique. I use the table of contents to drive my book's creation. What I mean is a table of contents is simply the high points of my book after I've completed the subject matter brain storming session.

I recommend once the brainstorming process get started, that you devote your full attention to each aspect of your life, while you are working that task. When you are with your family and other commitments, be there all the way. You'll foster the support you need when you devote your allotted time to your writing and marketing. The next part is to find a quiet or quieter place to concentrate and write your book. I find the writing process easier if I pre-plan my book. The bulk of the work I do in preparing my books takes place with a notebook and pen.

I do a lot of pre-planning in my head and outline a chapter on one side of a piece of paper. If my book is eight chapters long, I have eight pages of paper. I am a product of my times because my book plan looks like a PowerPoint presentation. I use bullet comments for chapter topics, supported by further bullet comments for the supporting ideas. Here is how I start a book:

- Start with book subject in mind
- Brainstorm keywords related to subject
- Group words into eight to ten topics
- Each topic is a chapter and words are paragraphs or sub chapters
- List a page per chapter in outline
- Develop out each page to complete written chapter

Start with book subject in mind

Let's work on a book together. We will tentatively call it *How to Write a Book.*

Brainstorm keywords related to subject

Our book topic brainstorm might be twenty to thirty words related to the subject I want to write about.

eBook, Paperback, Kindle, platform, audience, point of sale, advertising, attracting readers, time, family, Ingram Content Group, work, family, computer, paper, page count, friend, software, bookstore, how to find customers, tracking sales, advertising

Group words into eight to ten topics (we'll just do five)

Book format:
- *eBook*
- *Paperback*
- *Word count*
- *Page count*

Publishing Platform:
- *Ingram Content Group*
- *Amazon Kindle Publishing*

Time and Resources:
- *Family*
- *Friends*
- *Work*
- *Computer*
- *Software*

Platform or Audience:
- *How to find customers*
- *Bookstores*
- *Communicate book's existence*
- *Methods to attract readers*

Become a best selling author:
- *Point of sale*
- *Advertising*
- *Marketing*
- *Tracking statistics*

List a page per topic in outline

Develop each topic into it's own page header. Separate each topic by a unique page space. Each topic and following bullets as listed above will be its individual page.

Develop out each page to complete written chapter

Expand on each bullet adding sentences, paragraphs and sections. Pretty soon one page will turn into multiple pages and each section will become a chapter.

]I've planned books on my back porch table while watching my children play on the swing set. Slow times of the day also provide good opportunities to draft book outlines, and I've even sought inspiration while jogging. The point is book outline design doesn't demand more than a few sheets of paper and focus. Learn to manage time well, respect your commitments, and don't over schedule your valuable time.

Once I have chapters outlined I begin to write, and move to a quieter location. I have a desk where I create while everyone is asleep. However, I also have a laptop that I use when traveling and take advantage of airport, airplane, and hotel time.

Book Chapters

Your chapters should stand alone. As your book is a complete message, so should each chapter relay a complete thought. You may be closer to your book than you think, especially if you have been writing article or populating blogs. Or if you've completed a book already, you can do the opposite and use a completed manuscript as a source for blogs, training, and newsletters. This is a great way to draw attention to your book and an excellent marketing tool. Just write an article and refer to your book as the source. Apply a link to your site in your biography, and interested parties can visit your site and buy your book. I'll be doing the same for this book.

Use the Bottom Line Up Front (BLUF) technique and it works each time. Some publishers have an introduction section for each chapter. This works great, as long as the effort is taken to insert the BLUF at the beginning. Some authors fail, forcing the reader to search for the thesis or main point. Make it easy for your readers to see what you are trying to tell them.

I like to use introductions and summaries in my chapters. They help me to develop a chapter based story and set the direction for the reader. I recommend an introduction of the topic or what you intend to tell your reader, what you want to tell the reader, and then a summary of what you told the reader. The introduction can be in a simple paragraph or two. Sum it up in an easy to understand manner so that the reader fully understands what he or she will gain from reading further.

The next part of your chapter will be the longest. It's the part where you explain your message. This should be well organized into subtopics to keep both you and the reader on track. If you are writing a "how to" book, your chapter is just a small part of the how to process. For example, if your book is called *The Amateur's Guide to Photographing Babies*, then one of your chapters may be called *Keep Baby Smiling*. The introduction may start with, "In this chapter, you'll learn some great techniques to keep babies and their parents calm during the photo shoot." The rest of the chapter may have subheadings covering topics such as keeping mom relaxed, how to use your voice to get a smile, stinky is happy (don't rush to change the diaper if baby is smiling), and using toys to get smiles. Under each subheading you can begin to write stand-alone sections. Each section should use BLUF and then get into what you want to instruct and then finish with the summary. Using these mini-sections is a convenient way to provide small articles or blog posts.

Writing your book section by section, chapter by chapter

While writing your book, make each chapter a separate file. Instead of making one large document file, break up your manuscript into separate files with each chapter saved as a file. This will help keep your files organized and poised for formatting. Also, save the front matter (including the blank pages and all material following thereafter until just before the table of contents) as a separate file. You should not produce the table of contents and the index until everything has been completed, including several rounds of editing.

When you have a complete manuscript, proof-read, edited and ready to publish, build the ToC. The "References" tab includes everything an author needs to make a complete and professional manuscript. At this point, many publishers accept documents created in Word format. Even if you have not decided to how-to publish (traditional, niche or self-publishing), you will waste no time by using Microsoft Word applications. The software is inexpensive and this book will give some formatting pointers. If you do decide to self-publish, you will have a prepared document ready to convert to either Adobe Acrobat for submission to the printers, online book publishers, or to move into a professional software like Adobe InDesign. As a self-publisher, format is your decision. I have yet to read one review that tackles the choice of publishing software or book design quality. Good reviews are written about how well a book topic meets a need.

Developing Your Manuscript

During the first few drafts of your manuscript, you might not have full vision of your final product's design. After all, a draft will end up being well edited and re-written. Chapters and sections may be moved around or you may discover new writing topics. Once you have the manuscript ready, you can begin to formalize your chapter and section titles. Formatting the chapter and section titles into headers at this point will provide the foundation for creating the table of contents and index.

Start with formatting your manuscript. I've used several formats to write my books. For the sake of lesson consistency, I'll teach you how to use the format that I've used on other books. I prefer to use Georgia font for the bulk of the manuscript.

Next, set up the format of paragraphs. I prefer to justify which keeps the edges uniform but may cause letters to spread more than normal causing some sentences to look stretched or oddly spaced. This technique has been used in other books that I've read. You can also perform a hard return (Select "Enter") to send parts of the stretched sentence to a new line. You can play with this and pick out the best way to pursue the problem. If the stretch is no problem for you, it may not be a problem for your readers.

Take a look at most nonfiction books. On my shelf, all books have the same characteristics as I've recommended earlier for the front matter. Chapters should begin a third of the way down the page. You can use a chapter title if you wish. To avoid confusing the reader, begin with the number, hit enter, and put the chapter title. For the chapter title, use the "Title" option in the Styles section. This will tag your document and allow the easy construction of a table of contents.

I like to begin each chapter on an odd numbered page. Book chapters are constructed in various ways with chapter and section titles, page numbers, headers, and footers all depending on the publisher and editor discretion. There is not an industry standard or reason to believe that one style should be preferred over another. Choose the format you prefer and mimic it.

Combining each chapter into a complete manuscript

Once your book is ready to print, you will bring your individual chapters together into one document. Each chapter should be formatted consistently so that you can bring them together and keep the page numbers and headers flowing correctly. Experiment with your book to ensure your margins are acceptable. More white space and larger letters make reading more enjoyable.

 Select the layout tab for access to margins. Both Ingram Content Group and Kindle Direct Publishing (KDP) recommends a margin of at least 0.50 in. (13.0 mm) to prevent the text from being cut out during the printing process. I set my margins to be larger as I prefer more white space.

Unless your book requires otherwise, set the orientation for portrait. Next, be sure "Pages" are set for "Mirror Images". This will ensure the margins are legible on the bound side of the book. In other words, the margins will be unique to each page depending on whether or not it is bound on the left or right side of the page.

Also, determine the preferred book manuscript size. The print version of this particular book is 6 in. x 9 in.

Ensure each section starts with "New Page" to again allow proper page numbering when you add the header and/or footer.

Most books have the same format in common

I'll explain the important parts of most book manuscripts. However, if you would like to see an example, flip to the appropriate parts of this book. The very first page with writing should begin on the right hand side of the opened book. Many readers of nonfiction may use these pages to keep notes about what they are reading. I particularly enjoy marking up books and making my own reference notes as I devour it. I usually write a topic and page number of something that catches my attention.

The next page is the praise section of your book and other relevant books. If you've received glowing reviews, put them here. A book that has been reviewed gives the perception that it is endorsed at some level. You can request reviews from students, readers of your blogs and newsletters, or any number of people in your platform before you even write the book. You can solicit reviews from colleagues and customers once your drafts are finished. I also include a hyperlink to the book titles. For example, for my security books, I include reviews for the other security books and the hyperlink to those books so the reader can easily find it.

Title page

The next odd page is the title page. It is just a lone page with the title standing out in big bold letters. Start about a quarter of the way down the page and put the title in large letters. Make sure to use an easy to read, large, bold font like Georgia, because it just stands out. The reverse page should be blank.

Publisher page

The next odd page should again include the title at the same location, a fourth of the way down. Put the author's name about three spaces under the title. At the last fourth of the page, place the publisher information at the same size font as the author's name. You can put the publisher's address, website, logo, or anything you wish. This page is where the title, author, and publisher information pop out to greet the reader. You want to make all relevant information a memorable experience. Finally, add a graphic or a feature from your cover.

Copyright page

The next even page is where the publisher lists all the copyright information. It may be lengthy, so allow yourself plenty of space using an easy to read font small enough to fit all of it on one page. Always start at the top. I use Century Schoolbook or Minion Pro for this page. List the title on one row, the publisher's logo on the next. Press "Enter" two times and put the copyright information. This is the year that you file your book with the Library of Congress (Library of Congress and ISBN information is covered later).

Press "Enter" two more times and put your copyright statement. Take a look at the front pages of this book to see how I did it. Depending on your book, they may be different. If your book includes trademarks and logos or other branding, you may want to include statements that address copyright and ownership issues.

The rest of the page includes the ISBN and LCCN.

Thank You and Free Gift

Right after the copyright page I usually insert the free gift option, the thank you note for purchasing my book and a way to contact me.

Dedication

The next even page is the Dedication Page. There you can list all the people who you are thankful for in helping you get published. Do you have a hero or someone you respect? Name them here. Don't forget friends and family members or others who mean something to you, as long as they don't mind being included in the book.

Table of Contents

The next odd page is the Table of Contents (ToC). Manuscripts change so much during the editing process. Just put a placeholder here and complete it once the book is ready to print. ToCs can be created automatically with Microsoft Word or Adobe Indesign. Just format the chapter heading as a Title or Header and the software will read it and create your ToC.

To build a table of contents in Microsoft Word, just create chaper titles and put them into a Header or Title format by selecting from the home tab. Once your book is complete, you can select *Reference* and then *Table of Contents*. Then you can build a Table of Contents page based off the chapter titles. Chapter sections or anything else you want to be included in the ToC can also be added if you label them as a Header.

Beginning with Chapter 1, highlight the chapter titles using the mouse cursor. Next, in the header select "Title." The "Title" option will tag the chapter title for the table of contents. Next, scroll down your manuscript until you get to a section heading. If you have subsections, use the "Heading 1." If you have additional sub-subsections under that subsection, use "Heading 2" and so on. This will continue to update your ToC if you wish to include the subsection titles.

Next, select "References" on the MS Word toolbar. Then select "Table of Contents" and select the type of ToC that you want to display. Once selected, MS Word will format your manuscript and assign page numbers and build the table of contents.

Decide where page one will start. You can begin on the very first page of your manuscript or have the page count start on the first page of the first chapter. Then MS Word's ToC function will mark all identified headings and create a ToC .

Main Body

The next odd page will be the start of your manuscript. You will add this after the book is completely edited and ready for print.

Header/Footer

When you are ready to take on the print book, the rest of this section describes the way forward. Each page, except the first page of each chapter, should have a page number header. Chapter title pages do contain the chapter title in the main body before continuing right into the text, but headers with page numbers go on the following pages. If a chapter ends on an odd page, place a blank page so that the next chapter begins on an odd numbered page with no header.

You can build page headers that look similar to those used by traditional publishers. Use a different header for even pages and odd pages. This will allow page numbers to appear in a uniform area such as the inner or outer parts of the page. Also, your even number pages could be set up to feature the book title or author's name with the page number. The odd pages could have the chapter title with the page number.

Index

The index, if included, comes after the main body allows the reader to find what they want from the book. It provides more information than the table of contents and lists keywords by page number. The index is also completed once the manuscript is ready for print. I'll show you how to do this later.

To build an index, select the "References" tab. As you go through your manuscript of combined chapters, begin to highlight words that you want to include in the index. After you highlight a word with your cursor, select "Mark Entry" and a new menu will appear. In this example, I chose the word "Dog." I have the option to just mark this particular word once, or mark the word throughout the manuscript. If you select "Mark", only the highlighted word will be marked. If you select "Mark All", every time the word Dog is used, it will be indexed.

Select accordingly as it is important to discriminate times you want to index a word. For example, suppose your manuscript has Dog as both a noun and a verb. If your book is about animals, you would want to be selective of which use of Dog to index. You might index the word Dog in the following sentence: "Dog is man's best friend." However, you would not want to index the word Dog in the following sentence: "The extreme heat seemed to dog the antelope."

Remember to complete your index before you complete the table of contents. The index may add many more pages to your book and will throw off the page count. If you create a table of contents first, simply update the table of contents and the pages will reflect accurately.

Commonly Used Acronyms

A lot of professional organizations, businesses, and hobbyists have their own acronyms. Provide a list of commonly used acronyms from your book.

About the Author

The very next odd number page is the About the Author page. You can write about all the wonderful things you have accomplished in relation to the book's topic. If you teach classes, hold an elected position, or have a related job or responsibility, list it here. Also include awards and other accolades. You might also list education and certification if relevant. Include all books if this is not your only publication. An author with prior works is easily accepted as an expert and the listing could improve the sales of your previously published books.

I like to include an about the author section at the end of the book to be more personal.

About the Publisher

This is the last page of the book. Here you can list all the books and products available on your website and bookstores.

If you liked this book, then you'll like_____

If you have more than one book, then bring attention to the other books with the if this, then that discussion.

I have a favor

It will also be helpful to request the readers to post a review on Amazon. Amazon will only allow customers who make purchases from Amazon.com to make reviews I like to include the website address where the review will actually be written. It makes it easier for the reader. For eBooks, I like to have the hyperlink live so that they can navigate right to it.

Book Title

Consider waiting until finishing your manuscript before assigning a title. A working title is great for a temporary product, but don't commit to one until the final edit. The title may just make your sales, so make sure it is perfect. Allow others to read your book and suggest titles. I've often held contests to name my book. The prize includes a free copy of the book, as well as their name mentioned in the remarks. Your title should also contain keywords describing the book content. These keywords are very important for helping others find your book when they conduct a search.

It's best to use specific keywords in a niche market. Too broad and you will not be effective. It's a great practice to narrow the scope with a precise title rich in keywords, but for a small niche. For example, in my certification book, I use the specific certification in the title: *ISP Certification and ISOC Master Exam Prep.* If I try to use a broader "security certification" title, I would attract a wider but unqualified audience. I would waste their time as well as water down search results.

Book cover

Book covers are the most important point of sale item for any book. If funds are available, consider hiring a professional to design the cover. The book's cover is where the author and publisher may spend a good portion of their budget. Having said that, consider revenue predictions prior to sinking a lot of money into a cover. It does not help to spend up to $2,000 for a book that is not expected to generate five times the cost. Writing and publishing does not work well if the business does not turn a significant profit.

In the beginning, I have designed my own covers and I address how I did so in the paragraphs that follow. I now hire others to design my covers. There, you can find artists to bid on your project. I will be using such services in the future.

There are ways to have a professional product without spending a lot of money. My book on security certification was meant for a small audience. I could not afford to spend a lot of money on the design.

Also, at the time I did not have the money to buy book design software such as Adobe InDesign. InDesign, Qwark and similar software is required to generate a cover acceptable by printing companies like Ingram Content Group.

I designed my first book's cover myself with Microsoft PowerPoint. I then contacted a book cover designer I had connected with on LinkedIn and asked him to convert my design into an acceptable format. They graciously improved the design and provided a workable solution for under $100.00. I've since purchased Adobe InDesign, and now generate my own book covers. I've created over ten book designs and it was well worth the money. There are also stock photo websites that will allow you to purchase high quality artwork and pictures for book covers.

I continue to design book covers for my small niche subject matter because the market supports it. However, I expect to sell this book to a larger audience and will be spending the required amount for a professionally executed book cover design. For non-fiction books, a well designed cover complements a strong editorial description. A book's subject matter should be backed up by a solid cover reflecting the subject matter. The cover should be designed well enough for the customer to be emotionally moved to purchase. Book cover designs should not cause the customer embarrassment or shame when they buy it; avoid offending potential customers.

Book cover designs should match the content of the book or the subject matter. Books about model airplanes feature airplanes, modeling paint, glue or some supporting graphics. To feature anything other than words and graphics that support the content may negatively affect sales.

If your audience is professional, avoid whimsy. If your audience is fun loving, avoid cover designs that portray somber tones. Book covers in a niche could mimic other book designs of that and parallel niches. Feel free to research popular book covers that may apply to your specialized areas. Borrow from a bestselling theme and apply it to your book. For example, my books with US Army topics reflect the latest army combat uniform camouflage pattern.

If you plan to publish many titles, consider having a theme for each subject. Following my earlier example, all of my US Army books have a similar cover, the camouflage pattern. I just issue a new title and a different graphic. My security related books have a dark blue background. This association by book topic will make your design process easier, as well as help brand your company and books. Cross niche books are then easier for the customer to recognize and for you as the publisher to market.

The finished book cover should be legible while displayed as a small thumbnail photo. This is the ultimate test. Since your book will probably not be featured in a book store or library shelf, use the thumbnail test. *Amazon.com*, your website, *Barnesandnoble.com* and other online resources will feature your book as a thumbnail photo. These are very small and, therefore, should be legible. Letters and graphics should be clear and able to entice the potential customer to click for a larger image or more information.

Book covers should reflect professional quality. Things to consider are whether or not your book cover shows dirt stains or fingerprints. Dark colors will show fingerprints, while light colors will not. However, light colors will show dirt more than dark colors.

Fonts should be large enough to read on a thumbnail and in a complementary color to the rest of the cover design. Don't be tempted to get too fancy with the font. Fancy fonts can be distracting, and special effects can take away from the quality of the design and may not show up well in a small thumbnail photo.

Graphics and pictures should be of high quality. There are several sToCk photo websites where you can purchase royalty free pictures of high quality. ClipArt and other pictures are of low quality and may look cheap in a book cover design. Go for quality when you have the choice. Finally, make sure your words, graphics, and other design features align properly. Nothing says amateur more than misaligned and off center designs.

Don't forget to notify your public by updating your blog, articles, and social networking sites on your progress. The intent is to build a following of faithful readers who will buy your published book. By releasing short summaries of your topics, you can build interest. Even if you don't have loyal readers, at least those on your social networking pages will be able to recognize your name and associate you with your expertise. Also, update your newsletter and keep building up the reader subscriber database.

SETTING WRITING GOALS

Your book might not be published and you may not yet have the customers necessary for great sales. You probably have full time jobs, travel regularly, have a family that needs your love and attention, and chores and responsibilities at home and in the community. Pace yourself. Setting goals and milestones is incredibly important. However, the nervous breakdown that follows too tough of a schedule is never worth it. Never write a book or build a business at the cost of your job, health, or family.

Schedule

Get buy in from the family. Since writing will be after work hours (unless you have a really understanding boss), you will probably write in the mornings or after everyone else goes to bed. This addition to your schedule will add stress to your life. Part of your planning should be getting an agreement with anyone you are committed to. The agreement should benefit everyone. Families and relationships need love, communication, and patience.

Commitments to the community, church, clubs, and social organizations are also important. Let everyone know that you may have to rearrange your schedule, cut down on some events, or otherwise make yourself available to writing until you finish the project. Be sure to give something in return. It's not all about you.

Summary

This chapter has covered sources for researching excellent book ideas. It has also shown how to organize your thoughts and put them into a finished product and ideas on how to format your book. Following these suggestions may help you create a book by having more focus and spending less energy without sacrificing everything else. In the next chapter, I will show you why you should and how to self-publish your book.

CHAPTER 6 BECOME A SELF-PUBLISHING ENTITY

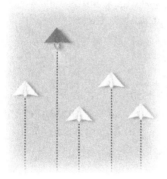

Introduction

Self-publishing provides an increasingly valuable method of getting information to your audience. With self-publishing, you can write, outsource the printing, and market your book while controlling the process. This type of publishing can be done with very little money up front and, if done right, creates a great source of revenue.

If you plan to self-publish, you will need some basic items and information. Books should have copyright protection and each book sold through distribution channels will need International Standard Book Numbers (ISBN). However, with Kindle Direct Publishing (KDP), there's no need to have an ISBN as they will provide one for you. KDP will also act as a publisher, not requiring the author to do much else other than prepare and upload their books.

If you write multiple books, you might consider starting a publishing company. It's not necessary to do so, but if this is something you are interested in, read further. If not, you can skip to the next sections and submit to KDP one book at a time.

In this chapter, you will learn how to create your own publishing company and determine what type of company structure is right for you. If you already have a prepared manuscript, you will learn how to establish an account with Ingram Content or KDP, both well experienced with supporting small publishers. Then we'll address profitable non-print products. These will help you reach a broader audience and possibly increase sales, as well as make your book more affordable.

Why self-publishing? Frankly, it may be your best option depending on the size of your market and the amount of money you can earn. When you self-publish, you do not receive author royalties, you receive payment for the books.

As I explained earlier, many traditional publishers may consider your niche market too small, and they may not have inroads into your specialized area. That leaves you with the opportunity to blaze the trail writing and publishing what you know best. During the past few years, I had originally built my business model after traditional publishing, attempting to capture their markets. However, I am changing to more of a self-publishing mode that relies on different publishing and marketing styles.

Having said that, you might consider reading the rest of this section on designing and starting your own business. Your book will provide you incredible opportunities and your readers may be seeking out your service. Starting a business can help you transition to providing that service.

CREATE YOUR OWN COMPANY

If you choose to create your own publishing company, you might be surprised how easy the set-up is. I started my journey after trying to get a colleague of mine to publish my book with his company. I am so glad he declined and led me through the process. It is one thing to publish your own books and it's quite another to be responsible for publishing someone else's. When clients contact me to publish their book, I try to encourage them to publish themselves. However, many don't want the publishing experience and I take care of that for them.

For those who want to be part of the publishing process, I recommend starting a registered company. The first step is to create an entity. In the U.S., you can start a sole-proprietor company, Doing Business As (DBA), Limited Liability Corporations (LLC), Limited Liability Partnerships, or Corporations.

Business Structure

Sole Proprietorship

A Sole Proprietorship is a business owned by one individual. The owner is in control of all equipment, supplies, and assets of the business. As a result, they receive all the money earned. They control all decisions and are ultimately the one entity who can commit the business to decisions. The upside is the same as with choosing to self-publish: the owner receives all the benefits and earnings that come with publishing. Owners enjoy full control over their books, including creativity, marketing, and sales.

The downside to a sole proprietorship is that the owner is ultimately responsible for funding the business. They are also liable for any obligations that may extend beyond the business into personal assets. This could be tough if any lawsuits are brought up against the company. It's possible that the owner could pay dearly for issues such as copyright violations or lawsuits stemming from business practices. Additionally, if the owner dies, so does the business. The business depends on the owner's involvement and the owner depends on the business to succeed.

Partnership

Partnerships exist when two or more people or businesses form a business entity. The partnership is a legal body put together for limited purposes. The partnership formed is independent of the individuals engaged in the partnership, and the organizations that form a partnership are a new entity. Depending on the type of partnership, the new entity receives the rewards, benefits, and liability of business decisions. Individuals are not liable.

Partners make the day to day decisions. This works well when partners are of the same mind and have the same goals. It can be a frustrating experience when these goals are not clear, personalities conflict, and creativity is stifled. Book decisions may not be in the author's hands, depending on how much authority the partners have in decision making. If you form a partnership, outline the duties ahead of time to determine who is responsible for creativity, marketing, sales, and other business decisions. You can split the decision equitably. In a partnership, more than one person is a stakeholder.

Corporation

A corporation is a business owned by one or more legal entities. The entities can be other corporations, businesses, individuals, or partnerships. The corporate entities are separate from the individuals who make up that corporation. Corporations offer the best legal protection, as the corporation, and not the individuals, is accountable. Likewise, all success and failure affects the corporation and not the individual. The owners and shareholders of corporations are those who own stocks. Each shareholder owns a percentage of the company, depending on amount of stocks owned.

Decision making begins with the election of a board of directors. This board of directors determines the direction and strategy. They hire and appoint company officers to take care of the day to day work. Presidents, Chief Operation Officers, Chief Executive Officers,

Vice-Presidents and so on are hired by the board of directors. Decision making for books will be determined by what is best for the organization and shareholders, not necessarily what the author wants. If you form a corporation, you may be giving up a large portion of your decision making, depending on the enterprises structure.

Limited Liability Company (LLC)

An LLC offers similar benefits and protection as a corporation, and the individual in an LLC is better protected than with a sole proprietorship or a DBA. The company is controlled by one or more owners. These owners can be individuals, corporations, or other LLCs. The owners can control the company or the owners can appoint managers to control company operations.

Single owners get all the business making decisions that come from a DBA as well as protection enjoyed by corporations. With partner LLCs, any of the owners or designated managers can obligate the company. However, owners are not personally liable for business debts.

Choose a Good Name

Since your company may go on to do great things, pick a name that is easily recognizable and easy to pronounce. Some companies have very long names that are difficult to pronounce. Avoid this mistake if at all possible. If you want your company to have your name or you chose a name that is difficult for others to spell or pronounce, consider using an acronym. Companies such as BAE Systems, IBM, BMW, and many more use this technique. They are well branded and the acronyms work since the names are unfamiliar to the worldwide audience, are a formation of many names, or for various other reasons.

Many authors and entrepreneurs have named books and companies with the first letters as close to the beginning of the alphabet as possible. This makes great sense, as lists are almost always alphabetical. However, if it's not possible, go with something easily recognizable, and easy to pronounce and write. I named my company Red Bike Publishing, LLC simply because one of my children used the name Bike Red as a username for their favorite website login. I also want the option of turning the company over to my children when they get older, or to be able to sell the company. Red Bike Publishing, LLC is not at the beginning of the alphabet, but the name is fun and easy to recognize and write. The title also generates a lot of interest.

Print on Demand (POD)

Self-publishing with KDP and Ingram Content are considered print on demand. POD keeps your costs down, as books are only printed when a customer places an order. The author does not have to buy hundreds of copies upfront and the services print, prepare and send books to the customer without the author being in the middle. With POD, a customer places an order for a book and the distributor prints and ships it to the indicated address. For example, when a customer orders your book from Amazon.com, Amazon.com notifies Ingram Content or KDP, depending on where the book is ordered, who then prints and ships the book. The distributor subtracts the printing and shipping costs from the order, and sends the remainder of the payment to the publisher, that's you.

POD also allows you to update your book information more frequently without having to worry about your inventory. For example, if your book information becomes suddenly outdated or a reader notifies you of a mistake in your book, you can simply upload a new file and the change takes place. The next books ordered will have the updates. With traditional printing, you will have to figure out what to do with the thousands of other books in your inventory. There are no worries or troubles with submitting new cover designs or updating book content. The distributor can also fill orders from the publisher. If you sell books straight from your website, want to send copies out to reviewers or professional organizations, or have several copies on hand, you can do so by placing an order. The distributor prints and packages the books using the publisher's address as the return address and creates a customized packing slip. Then they send the order directly to wherever you designate.

I use both KDP and Ingram Content for my publishing needs. In the beginning, I used Ingram Content as my business model had been to compete with traditional publishers. Now, I prefer Amazon KDP and use them heavily to market my book.

My experience is that with my security books, customers order in bulk through Ingram Content Group. Their distribution model typically supplies colleges, universities and professional organizations. KDP supplies the individual purchaser. So each provides value in its own way.

A word of caution. KDP may limit your ability to use other publishing platforms like Ingram Content Group. To prevent this, be sure to not choose worldwide distribution when setting up your title with KDP or make your book available with KDP after publishing with Ingram Content Group.

KDP

KDP is yet another option with less of a distribution reach, but has exclusive access to *Amazon.com*. There are no up-front setup costs and copies are less expensive than Ingram Content Group. The advantage is the access to selling and control of how books are listed on *Amazon. com* and their excellent marketing opportunities.

Set up a Title with KDP

KDP is built for the do-it-yourself publisher. Complete with tools and instructional videos and articles, KDP is an easy and fast way to get your books to market. When a publisher distributes through KDP, their books are always available on *Amazon.com*. KDP is *Amazon. com's* primary distributor which is one of the primary advantages. If you want to work and market exclusively through *Amazon.com*, KDP might be for you.

The beauty of KDP is that you can set up both print and eBooks and link them for better configuration management. They also have a new ability to print hardcover books. KDP provides excellent marketing tools that you can apply immediately to ensure your books success. I'll talk about specifics later.

To set up an account, visit:

https://kdp.amazon.com

Building your account and submitting your titles is simple and fast. KDP merges print version with Kindle eBook services. When you are ready to submit your books, just select "Add a new title" and fill in the provided spaces. Then upload your manuscripts and cover. The process is simple. Books and covers should be converted to Adobe PDF and then it's ready to go. Once uploaded and approved, your book will be listed as available on Kindle. Publishers can expect a royalty rate of between thirty-five percent and seventy percent from each Kindle sale.

You can upload your book and cover. Kindle does allow books to be submitted multiple formats. However, the best option is to download their Kindle Create App and import your book manuscript in MS Word format. Once upload is complete, you can review and approve the format. It takes a lot of work to format for Kindle but it may prove worthwhile. Many authors sell more Kindle books than they do print books.

KDP provides authors instructions on how to format print and Kindle books. They have downloadable templates for print and eBook formatting, cover design services and manuscript and cover upload instructions. Their learning library is very extensive. If you create an account you can begin learning immediately and publish your book when ready.

Cost of doing business

Though publishing with KDP has no upfront expenses, they do charge in the end. Authors can expect to pay 40% of the books' selling price for the experience of selling on Amazon. My titles on KDP provide less revenue than the same title I sell through Ingram Content Group. However, I do sell more titles with KDP.

Ingram Content Group

Though I prefer KDP at this time, I still use both Ingram Content Group and KDP. Ingram Content Group is an Ingram Books Content Company. That relationship makes it possible for those publishers who print with Ingram Content Group to have their books marketed to over thirty thousand wholesalers in 100 different countries, an excellent service for small publishers. Ingram Content Group prints and ships books. They also market books through their distribution channels with Baker and Taylor, Ingram, *Amazon.com*, Barnes and Noble and other Internet book stores and distributors. They do all the work and you, the niche publisher, control your product. In fact, some well-known traditional publishers are also using the print on demand technology provided by Ingram Content Group.

Setting up a Title with Ingram Content Group

Ingram Content Group is a great resource for small and large publishing companies who want to grow in the industry and distribute widely. When you register and set up your book title, you have control over the design of the cover, the interior of the book, price, and return policy. Ingram Content Group does require books and covers to be submitted in a particular format and provides excellent instructions on how to transform the book. In most cases, you just need Microsoft Word, a way to transform it into an Adobe PDF file for books. Submitted covers require a final design using Adobe InDesign, QuarkXPress, or EPS.

A publisher submits book information and books become available through the distribution channels to the world's booksellers and distributors. The wholesalers, retailers, and booksellers like Barnes and Noble and *Amazon.com* will provide them on display for their customers. In essence, Ingram Content Group takes the orders and provides the products. To get started, visit the Ingram Content Group website at:

http://www.Ingramcontent.com

Like KDP, Ingram Content Group facilitates an environment where authors can publish books in all formats and with different publishing options depending on needs and requirements. You can download all the operating manuals, instructions and all you desire to help you through the book publishing from book design to uploading the contents. The operating manuals describe book sizes available, how to submit covers and manuscripts, and other important information. The manuals are well written and explain everything necessary from start to finish.

Cost of doing business

You can register with Ingram Content Group and provide a title for less than $200 (this does not include the cost of ISBNs covered later). It is possible to begin making money without incurring any debt. **In fact, with Print to Order, your print costs are deducted after the purchase is made.** Once you establish an account and sign agreements, you can begin submitting titles. After you create your title, you will have a few options for providing the manuscript and cover for Ingram Content Group to begin printing. You can also set up eBooks.

Important Tools You May Need

The International Standard Book Number (ISBN)

The ISBN is a unique number assigned to books for cataloging and marketing. The thirteen digits identify the country of origin, the publisher, and the book. If you are interested in publishing a book that can be ordered online or through any one of thirty thousand distributors, get this number. A book is not required to have an ISBN. However, you will need an ISBN if you plan to make your book available through a supply chain system such as bookstores, wholesalers, and the Internet. ISBNs make up a numbering system or method of cataloging that helps others find your book; even the Internet can be used to find and order your book. With KDP, you do not need to purchase your own ISBN as they can assign one. Also, eBooks do not require an ISBN.

Each book title and format is unique and should have its own ISBN. Since customers can search for books using ISBN numbers, publish one title with an ISBN for the hardback, one for the paperback, one for each eBook format. Additionally, you would need an ISBN for significant revisions. It's possible that you could use almost a ten block of ISBNs on one title.

Corrections to spelling or small changes that customers won't notice may not need a new ISBN. However, create a new ISBN if changes are significant enough to cause customer concern with content or format. In other words, if two customers buy the same book, but they look totally different and one has more information, the other might feel jilted. If that's the case, get a new ISBN.

Bowker offers several options to purchase ISBNs. You can buy them as a single item or in groups of ten, five hundred, or one thousand for small publishers or up to one million for large publishers. I recommend buying at least a group of ten. You may or may not use all of them, but it is more economical if you plan on publishing more than one title and if you plan to have more than one format (print, eBook, audio recording, etc). If you plan on publishing more than three titles, consider the five hundred ISBN block order.

The Bowker website also lets you track your ISBN assignments on a digital spreadsheet. When you purchase your ISBN block, Bowker provides an online database to record and track your books. They will also invite you to create an online profile to track and update your ISBN assignments. Keeping up with multiple formats and titles requires a lot of attention.

Copyright

Protect your hard work and register books with the copyright office. You can copyright your work before it is published or even if you decide not to publish; it's your work and should remain your work.

Copyright doesn't protect the ideas, systems, or facts that the author uses in their works, but the way the author expresses the idea. In this book, for example, I don't own the methods that I write about, just how I express it. For example, an author cannot expect to protect a story about a worm eating an apple. However, they can protect the details, characters, and dialogue in the story. The rest of the world is free to write and protect their own stories of worms eating apples.

Consider the following paragraph as an example:

Amazon.com has rules for submitting books, Ingram Content Group is a good printer and has a system in place, social networking is a good way to market, and Twitter, LinkedIn and Facebook are some of the most popular. These are truths. If an author copied the way another author wrote their book, or completely reworded the book, that would be copyright infringement. However, fresh twists and new ideas are not copyrighted.

This book isn't meant as a pass to reprint the same old ideas, but to give fresh ideas that work in niche publishing. Some of the ideas presented in other books just don't work in niche markets. The methods are too expensive, unreasonable, and don't work when trying to reach a small audience. An author's job, in this case, is to provide a unique twist in available information and give fresh ideas for niche marketing and self-publishing purposes.

Feel free to use the ideas presented in this book to help you publish. I don't own the ideas. However, I do own the way I wrote the book. Whether or not I register with the copyright office, this book is protected from the time it goes on my keyboard into the computer storage. The formal copyright organizes and makes identification of the protected item easier. I can post my book online, in blogs, or through social networks, and it is protected.

The web is internationally accessible and it's difficult to tell if someone lifts my work and takes the credit. I am aware that others have used my security articles in book compilations and have not attributed credit. Professionals might use your articles in their blogs and will give you credit, as well as direct them to your website. As an author, you should respect others' works and assign credit to the original author if you use their words and works.

To register for a copyright, visit the copyright website and follow the instructions to create an account. An account allows you to see the status of submitted applications, create a profile, and register future works. Recently, the copyright office has replaced the traditional Forms TX for books, as well as the forms for works of art and sound recordings. You can register your copyright at:

http://www.copyright.gov

Catalog Options

Catalog options mentioned here are available only to United States (US) publishers with offices and staff in the US who are available to answer bibliographic questions about their books. The Library of Congress Control Number (LCCN) and Cataloging in Publication (CIP) are two well-known catalog systems. The CIP provides free distribution of pre-published and further distribution of completely published books to libraries and book vendors worldwide. The Pre-assigned Control Number (PCN) provides an abbreviated record, but is not further disseminated to libraries on the same scale as the CIP.

Here is a secret: you don't need all that. This book is primarily written for nonfiction authors who want to self-publish a professional book available to specialized organizations or professionals. It will most likely be available through *Amazon.com* and other online bookstores and distributors. This is the widest distribution effort and best marketing source.

You will most likely use print on demand and rely on word of mouth, social networking, non-traditional marketing and advertising, and keywords for search engines to let others know about your books. Once you develop your publishing company, you might only publish your books, and until you are ready to jump in full time, probably will not be publishing titles of other authors.

Additionally, if your book is well written and marketed, it will be successful and launch other books and products. However, according to the Library of Congress (LOC), the self-publishing model will make your initial books ineligible for the CIP and possibly the PCN.

The good news? You'll get calls from suppliers and vendors anyway. Many of my favorite books do not have CIPs. Some do not even have a PCN. Their copyright page just contains publisher and copyright data. As far as format and presentation, readers will not even know these numbers exist. They are only for mainstream distribution. The only reason they are necessary is to aid US Libraries and book vendors with a recording system.

Though the CIP is highly desired, the record is not necessary for a book to be successful. The LCCN/PCN may be available to you, but if not, you shouldn't be too concerned. Chances are, because of the niche subject matter, your book may not be eligible or desired for worldwide library distribution. If you would like to have catalog information, but are ineligible for LOC, you can always have a professional librarian research and provide catalog information for the copyright page.

In the event your book is eligible and your business model and subject matter supports wide library distribution, I'll list the options.

Cataloging in Publication (CIP)

The LOC assigns CIPs to catalog books in advance of publication. The purpose of the CIP is to provide catalog numbers for libraries. The publishing records are provided to libraries, book vendors and bibliographic services worldwide. This information is further disseminated to alert customers of upcoming books. The LOC sends CIP data repeatedly, updating the library community of available publications. This wide dissemination of bibliographic records is great publicity for the publisher.

Library of Congress Control Number (LCCN)

The LCCN is a unique number assigned by the LOC. It is used for creating records and cataloging titles in their library. Librarians use this number to look up books in the national database and self-published books for niche markets usually don't need an LCCN. Once a book is published, it is no longer eligible for the LCCN, so if you anticipate using an LCCN, order it before you publish. Since self-published books may not be eligible, the LOC can issue a number under the Pre-assigned Control Number program (PCN).

Pre-assigned Control Number (PCN)

Print on demand and self-published books are not eligible for the CIP that large publishers enjoy. The qualifications established by the LOC exclude publish on demand publishing categories. However, if you are a US book publisher who can list a publication address on the copyright page of your book and have an office capable of answering any questions about the title located within the US, the PCN is for you.

The PCN should be requested prior to publication. Once books are published, they are no longer eligible for a PCN. The PCN is also only for printed books. Electronic or eBooks are not eligible for the program. If you already have a book published without a library number, you can search the LOC catalog for the appropriate PCN. All books going through the copyright office are listed in their catalog. As long as your title has been processed by the copyright office, it should contain a number.

Summary

If you choose to self-publish, start early and get the required registrations and information as outlined in this book. Get the copyright early. If you plan to apply for the LCCN or CIP numbers, order them from the LOC. You can get these before your manuscript is complete. If you plan to sell your book through Ingram Content Group and other distributors, be sure to get your ISBNs.

Create your own publishing company paying particular attention to what type of company structure is right for you. Depending on your needs, you can form a sole proprietorship, LLC, or corporation. Explore your options and choose what fits your needs. If you already have a prepared manuscript, consider outsourcing the printing and publishing needs.

Review questions

What Kind of Author?

Answer the following questions with yes or no.

1. I want to write as part of my existing business.

2. I only want my books to represent my existing company.

3. I'm not interested in writing many books, but just want to use one or two books to increase my influence within my industry.

4. I'm not interested in publishing other people's books.

5. I'm not interested in starting a company.

If you answered yes to those questions, consider opening a KDP account and enjoy the freedom of being an author. Use KDP as an experiment to determine where you want your writing to go.

For no answers, keep going...

1. I have a lot of books and ideas that I would like to develop and market.

2. I have services that relate to my books that I want to develop and market.

If your answers are no, stop the process and publish with KDP.

If you answered yes, you should consider starting a business on the side, publishing with Ingram Content Group, and developing that business.

What kind of business?

1. I want complete artistic control of my books, titles, and covers.

2. I don't plan on having partners or employees. My plans are for a small company where I enjoy doing my own thing.

3. I'll probably just work out of my living room.

If you answered yes , consider starting a sole proprietorship, LLC, or S Corp, depending on how you want to structure your company regarding risk.

 If no, keep going.

1. I want my company to grow and hire employees.

2. I may take on partners.

3. I want others to be involved with business, publishing, and creative decisions.

4. If no, go back and consider starting a sole proprietorship, LLC, or S Corp, depending on how you want to structure your company regarding risk.

If yes, consider LLC, S Corp, or C Corp.

In all cases, consult an attorney, accountant, or someone with experience to help guide you through the process.

Name your company

1. If niche writing, what industry are you writing for? Consider using the industry somewhere in the name of your company.

2. Is your name well known? Maybe your company is named after you. After all, your name could be the genesis of your business.

CHAPTER 7 MARKET AND ADVERTISE WITH AMAZON

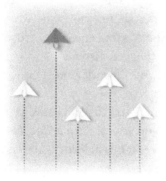

INTRODUCTION

With Amazon, there are two ways to market in my opinion. From an outsider point of view and from the insider point of view. An outsider is someone who has published books outside of Kindle Direct Publishing (KDP). They have published elsewhere, but their books are available on Amazon through the publisher's distribution channels.

An insider is someone who publishes their books through Amazon KDP and the books are in their full control to market through amazing KDP only possibilities. In this chapter, I want to draw a distinction between marketing with KDP and marketing with Amazon.

MARKETING WITH AMAZON.COM FROM AN OUTSIDER POINT OF VIEW

Marketing with Amazon is what any published author can do regardless of where book is published. This is a resource for everyone. The next section is a resource for only those who have used Amazon's KDP services. For this reason alone I would recommend adding KDP even if you are already using services with Ingram Content Group. Feel free to read and apply both sections to your marketing plan.

Your book on *Amazon.com* is your point of sale and is potentially your biggest online marketing resource. Driving traffic to your website, using search engines, newsletters, social networking, and blogs help reinforce your reputation as an expert and cause awareness for your books. With *Amazon.com* you also have another very important friend and, if you feed it well, it will work almost on its own to market your book for you. Your job is to ensure you keep your *Amazon.com* book page up to date with the information necessary to generate traffic from search engines. First, you will need to create an account with *Amazon.com*. This account makes it possible for you to purchase books, review books, and do great marketing.

If you have a book with an ISBN, it's probably already on *Amazon.com*. The rest is up to you. I've taught authors with multiple books to use this feature. Your books are there, now you be there.

At the top of the page, there is an option to either "Sign In To Get Personalized Recommendations" or "New Customer." If you don't have an account, select "New Customer." Next provide your email address and continue following the prompts. Once signed in, you will be able to create a bio and access the great marketing opportunities available.

Amazon.com Accounts

The following provides information to *Amazon.com* services and accounts that you should join to improve your point of sales and marketing performance:

Amazon.com Associates Account

An *Amazon.com* associates account is a must, as it provides a link from your website to your book site. When customers click on your book and buy it from *Amazon.com*, you will get a percentage of that sale in addition to the purchase price.

For example, my books are sold on *Amazon.com* as listed by the account I create through Ingram Content Group. When a book sells on *Amazon.com*, I receive a check for the books sold minus fees. My bestselling book has a suggested retail price of $59.95. When it sells on *Amazon.com*, Ingram Content Group prints and mails the book and subtracts the cost from my account. I pay the printing fees of $5.98 per book. That leaves the rest for me.

Cost to sell using *Amazon.com* associates account, figure in the following:

The math is $59.95 (Book price)-$5.98 (Printing fee) =$53.97 (Profit) + Associates fee. Amazon Associates accounts pay when you direct people to your book's page.

The Amazon.com Associates program (*Amazon.com* refers to it as "Associates" or "Affiliates" interchangeably) allows members to make up to fifteen percent in referral fees. I sell books on my website, and use my associates account to provide a link from my website to my *Amazon.com* book page. To do this, visit:

https://affiliate-program.amazon.com/

The Amazon.com Affiliates Stripe (Toolbar)

You can use the affiliate program to create brilliant marketing tools such as banners, widgets and other devices to add to your website. This in turns creates a buzz for you and your books.

Once you join, an Associates Site Stripe will appear each time you log on to your account. The Associates Site Stripe is a tool that *Amazon. com* has created to generate more sales for any of the books they list. You can take advantage of this to market and sell your books. You sell more books, *Amazon.com* is happy. If *Amazon.com* is happy, they will refer and help you sell more books, and so on.

The first option is "Links to this Page". Select the button and a window will open to demonstrate exactly how the link will appear on your website. Think of this as a shortcut to create a customized link to that page. You can post the link on your website and it sends traffic to *Amazon.com* for purchase. For an example, visit *http://www. redbikepublishing.com* and click on one of their book links. It will show information about a book and then a link to purchase the book on Amazon.

The interesting thing is while people are directed to *Amazon* to buy your books, you will also earn an associates fee for referring them to Amazon's store. Even if they buy other books after being directed to your book, you will also earn money. You can also make extra income by recommending related books and material on your website.

"Your Earnings Summary" is an important milestone indicator for how customers interact on your page. It is designed to show how many hits the *Amazon.com* page gets after being directed from the Associates link on your website and what they do once they land there. You can use these statistics to check how much you earn, how many items were shipped, miscellaneous referrals, how many clicks turned to purchases, and reports of types of links and how they performed.

You can get daily performance reports as well. The Earnings Summary demonstrates the website performance part of the story. While you may have statistics for your website performance and how successfully you drive traffic to your main page, this feature tells you what happens once customers click your website's *Amazon.com* book link. Do they buy your book, buy other books, or just leave? This milestone tool answers those questions.

Creating an Author Presence on Amazon

Create your Author Page

This is an account the author creates and updates. Describe yourself and your books. Provide your prospective customers with information and answer the following questions: What qualifies you as an expert? Why should customers buy your books? What are you up to now?

Author Central allows you to create an author centric page. To find Author Central, visit:

https://authorcentral.amazon.com

Follow all of the prompts to create your account. The Author Central page allows you to create an author profile, and update information in your profile and on your book pages. You can also maintain a blog on your Author Central page or link it to your current blog.

Author's Name

A book author's name is featured under the book title as a hyperlink. This links directly to your Author Central page. Put your computer's mouse cursor over your name and a window will appear that will allow you to access your Author Central page.

Select your title(s)

After you create your Author Page account, select your titles to be incorporated onto your page. This is done by clicking the "Add More Books" button. Once logged in, select the "Books" tab. A window will open allowing you to search your titles by author name, ISBN, or book title. Select your book and it will be added to your page. This is a great marketing technique, as anyone who looks at your page will discover more of your books.

Author Profile

Select the "Profile" tab. Your author bio will be profiled next to the book display of the author page. Make sure your bio provides any and all information that supports your claim as an expert. You want your audience to buy into your credibility and the *Amazon.com* Author Page bio creates that clout.

Here is my bio that I've written to establish myself as a security expert to better sell security books. I will modify the bio as books of different genres come out.

Jeffrey W. Bennett, ISP is the owner of Red Bike Publishing. A teacher at heart, he is board-certified in security, international exports, OSHA, and has a master's degree in Business Administration. Jeff is a former Army officer and speaks, writes, and provides products for small niche industries. Currently, his influence is in security. "Red Bike Publishing's Unofficial Guide to: ISP Certification-The Industrial Security Professional" provides security education and helps security specialists earn their certification. If you have a book idea that relates to a specialized area, please contact us at editor@redbikepublishing.com.

Jeff has traveled around the world and has met many peoples of various customs, celebrity, and influence. He speaks three languages and holds a Master of Acquisitions and Procurement Management from Webster University and an MBA from Columbia College. His experiences have involved adventure training, recruiting, world travel, diving, and flying.

Video

Select the "Video" tab to upload a video. Videos give your audience a chance to get to know the author. Smart phones and other devices now have movie cameras with decent quality. Also, there is affordable software available to help you integrate pictures, video, and presentations into video format. Rehearse a short presentation and upload it to your profile page, website, YouTube, and wherever you offer your books. You can see an example at my Author Central page.

https://www.amazon.com/Jeffrey-W-Bennett/e/B002BM2LY8

Events

If you have a book signing, webinar, presentation class, or other event, list it here. Your audience will be interested in what you are doing as a teacher and expert. If you are involved in your topic, you will come across as the expert.

Blog

If you have a blog, link your current blog with the Author Central blog. Whenever you update your blog, *Amazon.com* blog also updates. You can also post your blog articles one at a time. I choose not to link, but use the *Amazon.com* blog to feature my books and provide information about related books. This helps establish links to related books that might lead others back to your books.

Author Page for Marketing Research

Once you create your Author Central page, you can view it as a potential customer would. Go to your title and put the cursor over your name and a new window will appear. Click on "Visit (Your Name's) Author Page" and you will see how your page is set up. There is a ton of good information that you can exploit to determine the buying habits and interests of your customers.

Doing Research on your Book Pages

Customer Reviews

Return to your *Amazon.com* book title page, to see book reviews. If you don't have reviews yet, I'll show you how to solicit them. Reviews are listed in two places: under the author name and further down the page.

Book reviews are great marketing tools as readers who leave reviews market your book for you. Guess what? Reviews show up on search engines using keywords and phrases.

Happy customers are glad to write reviews, and good reviews sell books. Always ask for a review in your newsletter, blogs, websites, and social networks. I've been known to give complimentary copies to those who agree to leave reviews. Keep in mind that *Amazon.com* will only allow customers with an account to leave a review. If your reviewers don't have an account, they can't leave a review. I'd be happy to have you review my book if it has been helpful to you.

You can let industry experts know that they can use their review as a calling card by leaving their contact information. Only ask people to review if they have read and liked your book. It's unprofessional to leave reviews without reading books. Always insist that reviews are honest and flattering and be sure to request that a reviewer not leave a review if they did not like the book.

Book reviewers can also provide information about their own books. If you have a book and provide a review for a book on *Amazon.com*, you can insert your book's link. Just order related books, read them, and provide a helpful review. Buyers will notice your reviews and visit your site to find out more about your book. Once a purchase is made, *Amazon.com* provides the product pairing.

Frequently Bought Together

This is a great tool that shows what other books customers have purchased in addition to your title. The more cross purchasing is made, the more prominent the pairing will be displayed. Since my niche is so small, three of my books are often purchased together; that means tripled sales. Many customers who buy one of my books also purchase my related books and the relationship is featured for the world to see.

I am also fortunate to have one of my books purchased along with a book written by my publishing mentor, William Henderson, who inspired me to start my own publishing company. The keyword search has allowed both of our customer bases to see both of our books.

Customers discover similar books by keyword searches as well as additional information available on the *Amazon.com* book title page. *Amazon.com* uses customer information to recommend related books to raise their book sales. As more books sell, authors and publishers benefit.

Customers Who Bought This Item Also Bought

This is a similar tool used to show books and items that customers have bought in addition to your book. Once a purchase is made, Amazon. com includes the latest book to improve marketing and overall sales.

You can reference "Frequently Bought Together" and "Customers Who Bought This Item Also Bought" items to help your sales. These provide a listing of books that you can read and review to further bring awareness to your *Amazon.com* book page. All of the books I have reviewed are linked to mine. If you review a book on *Amazon. com*, place the review on your blog, web page, and wherever you post information. The relationship will be noticed, and more people will become aware of your book. The more your book is exposed, the better the sales. The better the sales, the more free marketing for you.

Editorial Comments

The editorial comments describe your book. If you print using Ingram Content Group or Kindle Direct Publishing (KDP), part of their service is to list your book on *Amazon.com*. The book description is featured here, however you can add so much more. Good reviews by satisfied customers are a great way to generate buzz and may sway a potential customer to make a purchase. It is best to have reviews in the review section. However, *Amazon.com* only allows legitimate *Amazon.*

com customers with accounts to generate reviews. If you send your book out for review, it is possible that some of your reviewers will not have *Amazon.com* accounts. Several of mine do not. To compensate, you can add their reviews and comments yourself to your title's editorial comments section.

Another option is to use your Ingram Content Group account. All you have to do is submit a book description change. To do so, log into your account. Next, put your computer's cursor on "My Library," then select "Title Information and Links." Enter the information to bring up your book. Once your title information appears, select "Submit Metadata Change." A new page will appear, allowing you to add to your book's description. Once submitted, your changes will appear on Internet bookstores.

> *Caution: When you use this method, always upload your complete description, not just an additional comment. Put the complete write-up. Otherwise, only the review will be posted. When using KDP, you can just add the latest comment and post it anywhere in the description.*

Product Details

This section lets your customer know about the size, page count, ISBN, weight, and other book details. The publisher enters book detail information when they create their title with Ingram Content Group. Amazon.com helps you market your book by letting potential buyers know how your book ranks by category. Out of all the books in Amazon's inventory, the number displayed is how your book ranks.

For example, one of my books is currently ranked at 83,830. However, rankings are further broken down into categories which are great niche topics. The category listed provides a better story. My book ranks a lot better in its individual category than in the overall rating. The better your book ranks and the more positive feedback on your book, the more your book will sell. Share the good news by putting your book's ranking on all of your blogs, websites, and social networking pages. You can do this by selecting the Facebook, Twitter, blog or other social network "Share" function available on your book's page. People in your network will visit just to see; they might even buy.

More About the Author

This leads back to your Author Central page.

Customers Viewing This Page May Be Interested in

Concerning sponsored links, this feature is an excellent way to research companies that might provide products or services in your genre. This section provides links to businesses that advertise on *Amazon.com*. Hopefully, these businesses relate to your book's topic. If so, click on the hyperlink and research the business, looking for opportunities for a possible partnership. Some ideas include asking them to link to your book, referring work to each other, providing books for their employees, and possibly subcontracting efforts.

Chances are that if your businesses are related, you can work together in a mutually beneficial relationship. I have been able to get book reviews, sponsorship, book sales, and other work through contacting like businesses. Some have even advertised on my website. They may also be able to expand your social networking contacts. Don't be shy about asking for help. I've been able to get business just by asking, "How can we help each other?"

What Do Customers Ultimately Buy After Viewing This Item?

This is a milestone that you can use to determine what customers do after visiting your book page. On the book's page is a list of books by percentage sold. This means that after viewing the book page, ___ percent of customers buy your book or competing books. The more of your books they buy, the greater the rating. The best thing that could happen is that your book is listed alone, selling 100%. The next best thing is that all of your other books are listed after the book displayed on the page. The worst news is if customers buy other books instead of yours.

If other books rank higher than yours, it means other customers are leaving your page to buy the other books. If that's the case, work on a plan to discover the reason and market your book better. Some issues could be the result of bad reviews or confusing editorial comments or book description. If your research indicates that is the problem, work on rewriting your book description and getting better reviews. Research the books that sell better than yours and see if there is any way to use your findings to generate more interest in your book. Look at competitors' tags, keywords, pricing, job description, reviews, and anything else that makes their books more appealing. Claim your page's market share.

Customer Reviews

Ask all of your customers to provide reviews. Reviews and ratings are prominently displayed on the book pages, so include a request for reviews in your book.

 If you liked anything about this book, please go to *Amazon.com* and provide a review. Your review will help others find this book and may help them to buy it. If you think this book will help others become experts in their niche, write, publish and market a book, let them know about it.

When someone leaves a review, thank them. I'll never forget the day an author contacted me to thank me for leaving a review. He even asked me for advice.

Look for Similar Books

The final features allow customers to look for similar books by subject and category. You can use this as a marketing plan to discover related books. Remember, the more books your book interacts with, the more exposure your book gets. Use these tools to find books in your subject and category. Take a look at customer reviews, book topics and descriptions. Interact in their communities and discussions. You can also use these tools to improve your book's description (what need are you meeting that is not being met by others) or to provide a basis for a new book idea (where a need is not currently being met). Have fun with *Amazon.com* features. *Amazon.com* wants to sell books, and you can use the features to help sell yours.

Track Sales Statistics with Amazon

To track sales statistics, you will need to create an author page and link all of your books to that author page. You can set up your account at *https://author.amazon.com/home.*

Once you set up your page, you can track sales data and determine where books are sold and the volume of books sold. You can also review your book sales rank and read customer reviews.

MARKETING WITH AMAZON FROM AN INSIDER POINT OF VIEW

Marketing and Advertising with KDP

Many years ago I did not publish with KDP. I relied on Ingram Content Group to put my book on Amazon's website. I would then rely on customers finding my book by luck or I could direct them to my book from my website. I did not care whether customers bought my book form Amazon, Barnes and Noble or anywhere else. There was no need to use Amazon at the time because the traditional publishing model was what everyone desired and self-publishing was for those of us who couldn't get traditionally published. However, many years later, Amazon became a champion of self-publishing authors. This allows for wonderful new marketing possibilities and helped create legitimacy for those who would become self-publishers. This is especially helpful for those of us who cater to small markets and don't desire to have our books in traditional books stores or libraries.

I want to draw a distinction between marketing with KDP and marketing with Amazon. Marketing with Amazon is what any author can do. However, marketing with KDP is only reserved for those who set up their titles specifically using Amazon's KDP services. For this reason alone, I would recommend adding KDP even if you are already using services with Ingram Content Group.

For example, with Amazon marketing, the best you can do is direct someone to your book from outside of Amazon. But once they get to Amazon, there isn't much you can do to help them find your book; you are an outsider.

KDP services makes you an insider. These services include the ability to market your book through exclusive opportunities. Where the marketing with Amazon section offers the ability to leverage books and other relationships to further your book, KDP allows you to actually direct potential customers to your specific book.

For example, if someone visits a bookstore they may know exactly which book they want to buy. They may have heard of the book by a referral, word of mouth or advertisement. In either case, they can enter the store and go directly to the book.

In another example, they may go to the exact shelf to find their book, only to notice there are other books related to theirs that may be additional options.

KDP marketing services allows you to virtually greet customers as they walk into the door and lead them to your book. It gives you the ability to find new customers, develop relationships with current customers and create ads to allow you to track return on investment.

KDP Marketing

Once you have uploaded and published your book using KDP, you can now take advantage of several publishing, marketing and tracking services that you won't have with Ingram Direct Publishing. For example, you can upload new content such as updated manuscripts and covers, change prices and markets, update the book description and so much more with immediate results and without cost.

To take full advantage of this opportunity, I recommend publishing Kindle books in addition to print books. Even if your customer base primarily supports print books. Besides being free, the additional potential revenue stream is worth the effort of formatting your print book for Kindle.

If you consider your print book to be a business card for your other products and services, then consider the Kindle version a pamphlet or marketing tool. KDP offers free marketing services specifically for the Kindle that the print versions will not have. That's what I do, I take advantage of marketing opportunities offered by KDP, using my Kindle promotion tools to bring customers to my print books.

However, these possibilities are only available when you enter your book into the Kindle Select program. Kindle select requires you to offer your eBook exclusively through Amazon KDP and no other eBook platforms. There are advantages to this exclusivity. You can get paid for each page customers read with their Kindle and your books will be available to members.

Once your books are up and ready for sale, you can market your books for free with Kindle Countdown and enroll in the exclusive Kindle select program. Kindle Countdown allows you to enter your Kindle version in a short period marketing plan at either a very reduced rate or free. During these Kindle promotions, Amazon will feature your books and increase visibility.

Amazon Ads

One of KDPs best features and the best reason I can think of to publish with Amazon is the ability to create ads specific to your book. By way of background, prior to 2020 I primarily published through Ingram Content Group and relied on them to distribute through all of their channels. My books always found their way on to the major websites. However, as mentioned earlier in this book, most of the advertising I tried on Linked In, Facebook, and other social media sites were just a waste of money. I spent hundreds of dollars for people to click on my ads and not even buy the books. A colossal waste of money and time.

However, when I discovered that I could advertise the books that I published with KDP, I realized that I had hit gold. I read all that I could from authors and vendors on Amazon.com who had already taken advantage of the opportunity. I attended classes and paid consultants to teach me their craft.

Finally I had learned enough and tailored what I had learned to fit my niche. Who would have thought that I could use ads to ONLY attract a handful of security professionals? I applied what I learned and immediately jumped from very few sales to hundreds of dollars in sales per month. For me, these are the only advertisements I will invest in. I am actually leading customers into the store, showing them the bookshelves where the books are and recommending other books. I can even wrap my multiple books into series ads.

Amazon Ads also allows you to collect, observe and respond to return on investment statistics such as how much you are spending, cost per click, and so much more. However as a word of warning, these ads can go horribly wrong. In the beginning, I sold $1000 worth of books for every $3000 in advertising costs; not a good return on investment. However, I learned many valuable lessons and last month

I earned $1600 in sales for $580 in advertising costs; a great return on investment. There are so many things to share and I plan to write in a new book very soon.

Track Sales Statistics with KDP

With KDP you can track your book sales success. All within the KDP dashboard, you can manage book uploads, update book details, track sales statistics and manage Amazon Ads all in one location. The Reports tab will allow you to access data such as number of books sold by title, author and date range. You can also review historical sales data, ad performance, payment history and so much more.

Summary

Successful marketing begins with a plan and a way to measure results. *Amazon* provides a great resource for authors to attract and sell books to customers. The page that features your book is full of information not only about your book, but of potential marketing avenues.

REVIEW QUESTIONS

1. List five keywords and five phrases related to your niche and your book.

2. Write a review of your own book or book idea. Use this as your book description.

3. Write five things that make you an expert in your niche. Form this into two paragraphs. This will be for your author bio.

CHAPTER 8 NICHE MARKETING

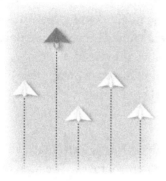

INTRODUCTION

This chapter will show you how to market your book without spending a ton of money. Niche publishers have a built in and focused audience which provides unique marketing advantages. Since you already know your audience, you can aim marketing directly at where they shop for books, search the web, or at other activities.

SETTING MILESTONES

Setting milestones is one of the most significant requirements of marketing. Milestones are markers that tell you where you are in relation to your destination. For example, if you are traveling from Boston, Massachusetts to Los Angeles, California, you should be reading the appropriate signs indicating the correct heading. Signs welcoming you to Canada or Mexico indicate you are headed in the wrong direction. Milestones let you know whether or not you are on track to reach your goals. Set goals and check your milestones often so that you don't miss your mark.

A few years ago, I was enjoying my hobby of flying. I loved to pilot an airplane, but discovered navigating required a huge amount of focus and talent. I never fully developed the skills required to maintain heading and usually ended up getting lost. Instead of enjoying the flight and relaxing, I continuously conducted situational awareness checks. Just as someone might count steps and look for obstacles as they walk somewhere, I tediously compared maps and instruments with the landscape below. If I veered off course, I wanted to know immediately. If I couldn't match my map with the ground, then I knew I wasn't flying where I thought I was. On this occasion, I wasn't following my plan.

 Half an hour after leaving North Carolina, a voice crackled over my headphones; it was the control tower. The man on the other end asked me where I was headed. I reminded him that I intended to land in Columbia, South Carolina. I went on to explain that I would continue to follow the route on the west heading of Interstate 10. He then told me that it would be hard to get there in my current heading, due south.

I had become focused on the wrong road and didn't read my instruments. As a result, I became disoriented and was following Interstate 95 toward Florida, instead of Interstate 10. He led me to the correct heading and I was back on track. The lesson is this: make a plan, follow your progress, and make necessary adjustments before you get lost. Losing in the publishing business could cost customers and market share.

I've led you through the mechanics of writing a book and the next question is can you market? Can you find your customers, make potential customers aware of your presence, create a burning desire for them to buy your book, and then close the sale? The entire success of marketing your book depends on continuous situational awareness research. Develop ways to measure how you will determine what you need to do to reach your clients, the message you want them to receive, and how you will create a need that compels them to buy. Then determine how you will grade your efforts along the way. Make sure it is a continuous process, and leave room to make adjustments without losing time and resources. Going on a journey without a plan and without the ability to check your progress will always get you lost.

I've spent years developing ways to recruit others and market concepts and products. I've learned one thing throughout my evolving education: no matter how great your book or product is, it will never sell if others don't know about it. Good marketing is behind every bestselling book's success and makes products bestsellers. New authors sometimes make the mistake of thinking that just because they write a book, others will flock to it. The flaw with that thinking is that there is just so much competition.

BUILD TRUST-BUILD A PLATFORM

Just because your book is the only one available, it doesn't mean people will buy it. No matter how hot the topic, you've still got to do the marketing of not only the book, but of yourself as the expert. Even if you have an incredible book, it will fail without the proper marketing.

Think of all the books you've read. Perhaps you've read some obscure books that you thought were incredible. You tell your friends about the reading experience and they give you a shrug; they've never heard of the book and therefore lack your passion. Somehow someone wrote a great book and it fell into your hands by accident.

Now, think of another situation where you've read a bestselling book. Advertising, word of mouth, reviews, and great marketing let you know it was available. You may have had an incredible desire to own the book. You finally receive the book and, with anticipation, you devour it. You find it is a good book, but perhaps not any better than the obscure book you had earlier fallen in love with.

The difference: good book plus good marketing equals terrific book sales. Good book plus bad marketing equals no sales. The message? Marketing is the single most impacting event determining a book's sales. Just writing a good book is not enough. Your customers will buy what they have a burning desire to own. Create a great product and an incredible marketing plan. Writing and publishing a book is financially inexpensive as some incredible and proven marketing techniques that I've used and recommend are free.

Traditional Advice Might Not work

The wrong kind of marketing will cause you to fail. Just as marketing without a plan will get you lost, marketing to the wrong customers will cost you time and money. Traditional advertising methods usually don't work for books. It is extremely treacherous when writing for a small, specialized audience. Think of the last time you heard of a book advertised over the radio, newspaper, television, or other media. Books are incredibly personal, and trying to use traditional advertising is just a waste of money. There are many out there asking you to do this. Someone is getting rich and it's not you.

You might be tempted to advertise locally in newspapers, on billboards, or on television. After all, that's what the other marketing experts recommend. They tell you that such advertising could result in celebrity status. It's tempting to think that broadcasting to such a large group can only result in great sales. I know the temptation and I've tried it. It just doesn't work. Paying large fees to advertise to two hundred thousand people when your target market is only three thousand potential customers is not good business. It's like throwing mud at the wall to see what sticks. It might help with awareness, but what is the general public going to do with information that is not useful to them?

What is effective is becoming a rock star in your specialized industry. That's what I've done with my small security niche. I've found a way to create awareness. Though the majority of the world doesn't know me, I am well known and respected within a certain national level professional organization. The funny thing is the fame has resulted from all the free campaigns I've done, never paying for advertising.

I've seen no results from some of the wasted funds committed to advertising and marketing meant for wide customer bases and more traditional products.

When is such traditional advertising effective? Let's look at others who successfully advertise using the traditional and mainstream media. They are successful because they have found a way to appeal to a massive audience. They can spend millions of dollars for premium advertising space knowing that their product will sell and they will recuperate the expenses. For example, everyone in the civilized world wears clothing, lives in some sort of dwelling, enjoys some form of entertainment, and expects a certain quality of life.

Watch TV, listen to the radio, and open a magazine. You will probably see similar types of products advertised. The products aren't typically being introduced for the first time to the market. Instead, similar products are jockeying for their position at the top of the sales within their category. Providers of household cleaning products, food and beverages, restaurants, automobiles, airlines and other products with mass appeal pay with confidence knowing their advertising will result in low risk sales. Chances are that the majority of viewers, listeners, and readers of the advertisements will have a legitimate need to buy the product. They will be able to measure a return on investment. Conversely, niche ideas will flop in these venues as it's too hard to find a customer.

Now, let's look at my products (just because I'm more familiar with them and how the public will receive them). I sell a very specialized product to such a small niche where the general public has no need for my product. The advertisement will be similar to throwing a handful of rocks trying to hit a tree with my eyes closed. If I hit, it will be entirely luck, and maybe at least one of the rocks might come close. You also don't want books returned when the wrong customers mistakenly buy them.

Niche marketers need more precise and focused efforts. They need a well-adjusted slingshot with an aim point and a reachable target to put the rock precisely where they want it.

There are also incredible numbers of businesses who are happy to take your money to help you advertise, market, or institute a public relations effort based on your book. They claim to help you get on the best television shows, in all the libraries, and on the most prominent bookshelves. Their marketing model may actually work for a few authors with a broad scope or topic. But that kind of marketing depends on a few things: how the book is published, the topic of the book, and the availability of the book.

As an author, you may receive email or see advertising inviting you to join a marketing initiative to get your book in bookstores or in the hands of librarians. You are asked for a description of your book, a picture of your cover, and some other information. Their plan is to email your book, along with several hundred others, to librarians and bookstores with the hope of yours being magically picked up and distributed worldwide. You get the strategy of hope for a small fee. But, hope is not a good strategy.

There are already a few strikes against this type of advertising. The first is that books are distributed through a process that self-published and print on demands are excluded from. Librarians and bookstores receive a book's information from the Library of Congress and distributors. If your book is not in the CIP process described earlier, chances are great that it will not be picked up by librarians and traditional bookstores.

Others take advantage of your hopes and dreams by claiming to have connections and inroads with major buyers. In fact, they collect your money, add your book information to a database with several hundred other authors, and email it to their points of contact. The points of contact may not even be a result of a personal relationship, but simply a collection of email addresses. You then are tied to the hope that somehow the recipient of the email is going to take to time to look at all the books and pick yours. The reality is librarians and bookstores already have an acquisitions system in place. Avoid this type of business, as all you will do is lose money.

It took a while for me to realize this. I've read tons of self-publishing and marketing books, paid for advertising to hundreds of thousands of recipients without realizing sales for those particular efforts. Many marketing leaders and authors earn a living writing about the success of Internet advertising. They claim that you should be buying mailing lists for libraries and bookstores, email campaigns, and magazines to successfully sell books. However, these methods just don't work and are non-applicable to niche marketing. Others claim that the Internet is an untapped gold mine and all you have to do is make a product, pay a fee, and sit back and collect millions of dollars.

Don't get me wrong. I am not trying to put down these services as they are, in and of themselves, not bad. However, they don't always work for niche marketing. In my experience, they just didn't target my market and their models were not appropriate for my niche. Before you spend money, be sure your audience is specifically targeted in the campaign.

Niche Marketing Failures

At this point I want to put your mind at rest. Though I have tried and failed at these traditional marketing efforts, I have been extremely successful with the techniques I will show you. Some of my books are ten years old, but still sell consistently and with great results.

This is where it gets dicey. I am recommending just the opposite of what all the marketing gurus are suggesting, but please read completely before you make a decision.

Google offers services to help you get to the top of the search engine results. You can advertise with them using Adwords or Pay Per Click. When customers use a keyword search, your website is featured prominently in the search engine results. Additionally, you can create an advertisement that displays in the search engine's results margins. When people click on either the advertisement or the search engine result, you pay the agreed upon rate. You can control how many times your information is displayed and how much you want to pay per display. If your site is prominent after a Google search, a customer may click on it. However, if your site does not offer the products the potential customer thought she would see, she will navigate away from your site but you still have to pay; quite a risky endeavor for a niche marketer.

For example, I sell security products and books to a discriminating customer base. In general, security has a lot of implications: home, event, executive protection, bank, commercial, financial, and more. In my case, my clients protect sensitive information. If I use pay per click to sell "security" products, I may see more and more potential customers visit, only to leave without making a purchase. Even if I use focused keywords, the wrong clients could still visit, costing my business money. If such advertising were to bring in paying clients, it still may not be enough business to warrant such efforts. My advertisement may show up at the top of all security searches surpassing the other vendors. However, if the customer is not looking for my product and has no use for my product, I've wasted his time and my money as he clicks through.

Facebook and LinkedIn are both excellent marketing venues, and they offer similar advertising opportunities as Google. Again, this doesn't translate into sales if you have a small, specialized market. Leave such advertising for those with more mass appeal. You've got other options that I'll show you in the next section.

Which works better, paid advertising or free Internet opportunities? I still think (and have the numbers to back it up) that informative and attractive blogs and newsletters provide the best marketing for your book. After all, you are the expert on your book and who better to talk about your book than you.

I recently ran an experiment with LinkedIn and Facebook. Against my better judgment, I reluctantly decided to once again pay to advertise my books and publishing company.

Using Facebook, I created four ads: three for books and one for Red Bike Publishing. Each ad is a pay per click ad and I set my limit to $10 a day. I gave each ad a max of a one hundred dollar limit before pausing it. I also limited my ads' exposure to demographics likely to buy my book.

For example, for my security clearance books, I set the ads to be visible for 22-55 years old and/or small business owners and/or professionals with technical backgrounds and living in the US. For my novel, I set it for women 18 years old and older, with interests in novels, eBooks and Christian fiction. I tailored each ad with carefully selected demographics.

I could tell the ads were enticing, as they received many clicks. I also saw my charges increasing significantly, but no sales. The ads rang up costs with no return on investment. You might argue that the audience did not like the link they clicked on, and I would agree with you.

The point is that it is incredibly hard to advertise niche books to the general public. The public might not understand what they are clicking on until they click. If they buy, great. If they don't, you're out a buck fifty. The ads provide just enough room for a sentence or two, not enough to really understand the product. Once they click, they can read more and either buy or move on.

Let's dig further. I went to Google Analytics to see how these ads were performing. Proving my point, I could see that though the audience clicked on my links to see the books, they did not buy. Now I realized that my advertising budget was going down the drain pretty quickly.

So, what does work? Providing informative articles. Looking back at Google Analytics, I see that all online sales were a result of referrals from my blogs. Out of the thousands of sales annually, I can tell you none came from advertising. That's why I rarely advertise unless to a specific industry related niche newsletter.

FREE STUFF THAT WORKS

Guess what, niche marketers can command top search engine results for free. Many marketing tools are available for you at no cost. Article writing and interacting on social media networks can result in top search engine rankings. Also, including keywords and phrases within your websites, blogs and newsletters that search engines pick up on really works. Your challenge is to find a possibly elusive market and send them the right message.

My market is hard to find; many in the security niche do not have an online presence and mailing lists aren't always available. By nature, members of some small security niches do not participate in social networking and limit Internet behavior activity.

However, what I have learned creates an advantage for niche marketers. All professionals have email addresses issued by their corporations, belong to professional organizations, and are hungry for education. I also know their varying experience levels and many are appointed to their positions as an additional duty. Though I can't find obvious personal contact information or a specific "security" presence, I can find them using non-traditional methods.

MARKETING TOOLS FOR NICHES

Whether or not you use all or some of the recommended ideas, ensure your efforts are all connected with one effort feeding the other. This is how you increase awareness while expending the little time and energy you may have available. Always have your point of sale at your website with links to your social networks, blogs, and other marketing and sales sites. Include your website, blog, and other places customers can find information about you in your email signature. As you send email, your signature block creates a buzz.

There are excellent ways to market and sell without spending money. Networking with professionals, attending seminars, writing articles, keeping blogs up to date, and making constructive use of the Internet can lead to sales, if done correctly.

Caution! Some of the ideas that follow are very addicting. You may get so caught up in the socializing that you take time away from writing and marketing. Follow these recommendations and develop a plan of action for how you will define and measure success. Otherwise, you will waste time and effort on mindless activities.

World class marketing can be easily executed by self-publishers and authors. It is one thing to be good at writing, know the self-publishing industry, and capable of getting books to market. It's quite another to become recognized as a leader in your niche industry, recruit assistance within the industry, and become recognized for the good work. In the second example, your efforts perpetuate themselves as you earn trust; others become force multipliers and quickly engage and support your vision. One way to ensure such success is to cross product market.

One way to do that is through professional branding. Alone, branding is not the answer to instant success, but does complete the picture. For example, there are many authors who are very influential and well respected; their work stands alone. Cross product marketing for them would continue to demonstrate their dedication to their industry, technical competence, and leadership.

Once you achieve a recognizable brand that your niche industry easily identifies with, the next step is to validate both the accomplishment and the certification. In other words, the stellar marketer can take the opportunity to demonstrate the importance of the brand and why customers should trust it. Once recognized, there are many ways marketers can capitalize on many opportunities to become better known and trusted.

Here are three ways your brand can become better known:

1. Send out a press release. News organizations are always looking for great articles. Newspapers have a mini-section where local industry can announce accomplishments. Write-ups should include your name, the organization you work for and the importance of your product. Don't just write that you wrote a book, but tell how the book is helpful to the industry.

2. Put the accomplishment under the "News" section of your publishing website or newsletter. This lends credibility to the work, and demonstrates that your organization values the work. This is great for self-publishers because they can talk up the value of the book and demonstrate how the publisher values the book.

3. Insert language into every blog, newsletter, post, or related books that mentions your other accomplishments and vice versa. For example, I always ensure our proposals include "Jeff is the author of _____" when providing bios, blogging, guest writing, or in writing new books.

I cross market with all of my products. This adds to the appeal, qualification, and professionalism and increases your presence as a publisher and author.

Branding is just another feather in the cap of the self-publisher and author. But without the demonstrated work ethic, capability, or effectiveness, branding is a wasted effort. However, pair it with quality books and publishing, and it provides a winning combination. As author and/or publisher you can equally benefit from each book.

Design a Logo

I recommend designing a logo that everyone understands and recognizes as your brand. Use it consistently on your products, marketing, and website. If you have the talent to design yourself, then go for it. If not, here are a few websites that I have used for logo and bookcover designs:

- fivrr.com
- 99designs.com
- 100covers.com

OTHER MARKETING OPTIONS

Set milestones for social media marketing to help you maintain focus. The following are samples of what I use. I have my favorite strategies based on results and these results get my full attention. I might continue to experiment with the ideas that don't work well, but only enough to test them. Spend your maximum effort on return on investment. Focusing on marketing that doesn't work doesn't make sense. Keep your emphasis on what works, improving on what is successful and ignoring everything else.

Marketing ideas published here have been tested and proven by others. Additionally, I have used them in my business model and during my M.B.A. studies, and have generated important branding and recognition leading to other business opportunities. **100% of these ideas have worked.**

Remember, your books are not designed to compete with large publishing house marketing and advertising. Niche marketers have a more defined audience and must focus efforts to reach them. Straying too far outside of the target market produces wasted effort. The following ideas are meant to help you find your target and join them where they are, or invite them to where you have a strong presence.

Complimentary books for special functions

Giving away books to niche or industry experts and peers is a sharp business idea. Complimentary books can be used to generate reviews and create excitement. Many people may not know your book is available and other marketing ideas may just not be reaching them. However, a free book in the hands of influential people causes discussion and others will seek to purchase their own copies. Books I've given have generated comments such as, "I didn't know this book was out," and "Why doesn't _____ organization sponsor it." When you send complimentary books, you only pay the printing and shipping and handling costs; not a big expense considering the outcome.

I belong to a professional organization where members in good standing are eligible to take the security certification. In the early days of my business, I bought advertising space. My sales built up slowly, but my research indicated that the advertising had little to do with sales results. When I stopped advertising, sales continued to grow.

I began contacting the organization's chapter chairpersons in each region and offered free books. I provided books to ten professional organizations for the same cost as one business card sized advertisement in the national newsletter. The result was tripling sales volume. I had my most successful sales month ever because of the buzz that developed from the giveaways. Additional benefits included more people signing up for my newsletter, and one chapter adopted my newsletter as theirs (they just forward my newsletter to all of their members).

Complimentary books for review purposes

Traditional book techniques include contacting national magazines and newspapers for reviews. This works successfully for books addressing broad genres and topics. However, such pursuits may be a waste of time for niche authors and publishers. Not to burst anyone's bubble, but requests for book reviews from the wrong source will not increase sales. This may come as a surprise, but if you think about it, spending a lot of time reaching reviewers whose audience will not benefit from your book will focus your efforts in the wrong direction.

For example, why would the New York Times run a review on a book called *The Proper Way to Assign a Combination to a Vault* or *How to Properly Align the Wheels of a Model Train*? Not that your book is not incredible, but what would a niche or specialized book offer the general population? National magazine reviews are for books that meet the needs of the general public.

Books for review should be sent to experts and influential people in your field. Requesting to have reviews posted in your book page at *Amazon.com* or in industry or hobby related blogs, websites, electronic newsletters, and print magazines and newsletters is an awesome strategy. A strategically placed, well written review can tip a potential customer's decision toward the purchase. Since I have several books on Amazon, I know that some of the subsequent purchases would not have occurred had it not been for the recommendation of well-known experts in the field. Reviews help books gain instant credibility and potential buyers may be finding the book for the first time.

Blog

Blogs, articles, or newsletter? All or one? You should decide where to put your efforts. Blogging is an easier option, as article sites don't give you as much freedom. For example, I've written blogs about applying Porter's Five Functions to Security and another one with application to publishing. However, the automated editing of article sites considers these duplicate articles, and wouldn't allow the article to be published. A computer made the decision even though each article had entirely different content. For reasons of freedom, ease and marketing, I prefer to use blogs.

I use BlogSpot, Wordpress and post on my own website. All methods provide good marketing options such as the ability to make blogs look like a webpage. They provide statistics that show how many times the blog is visited and how many comments are provided by readers, and allow readers to follow your posts.

Blogs are great for marketing and allow you to feature your books, products, and websites. Blogs can also link to your Facebook, Twitter, *Ezinearticles.com*, LinkedIn and others that might be applicable. When you post to your blog, it will also feed to the other sources. That way you spend your efforts writing great articles and posts knowing that it will be featured to your entire audience.

Post regularly, as you are able. The more you blog, the more you get noticed. The more informative your blog, the more sales you can achieve. Keep your blogs to the point, use bullet comments, and show your readers how to get something done. Three Simple Ways to...., Solve __ in Three Easy Steps, and Five Ways to Create More _____ are compelling titles, just be sure to deliver what you promise. Don't forget the point of sale or direct your readers to your point of sale.

"If you found this post useful, see more ideas in (name of your book) at: *www.yourwebsite.com*", or embed a hyperlink in your book title. I also put an Amazon Associates link to my book right in the article. I also feature pictures relevant to the article. Many times my book covers are perfect.

Newsletter

Newsletters are a great way to promote your products. I've laid out the format and distribution method for a newsletter, but let's talk about how to use it as a marketing tool. Offer something incredibly useful to your audience. After all, why would someone volunteer to let you have access to their email address?

Show them the benefit before they receive the product. If they agree to let you have access to their time, make sure it is worth their effort. I offer a written report related to the industry and study questions for the security exam. This is already something valuable and is related to hot topics in our industry. Potential customers now allow me to provide information and show them my products. Also, consider interviewing experts in your field and writing articles based on the interviews. Your audience will enjoy learning how these experts arrived at their current positions.

Put promotional company information in your newsletter. Your articles are the same as your blog posts so there is no extra work to do except format the newsletter setup. Newsletter or email services like *Icontact.com*, have automatic subscription capturing, forwarding capability, and other ways for your audience to sign up. Once people receive your newsletter, they will be exposed to great helpful niche articles as well as information about your book and products. You are presenting yourself as both an expert and a provider.

One way to promote your business is to include links to your website throughout the newsletter. While writing articles related to your niche, highlight a few keywords that link to your website selling your book. Dedicate space to feature your book cover with links to your website. Keep links fresh so that readers will go to your website as they are reminded to throughout your newsletter.

When someone joins my newsletter, they receive an automated response of an archived newsletter. Then a few days later, they receive a catalog of products. Next, they receive sample questions to help them study for the security certification. Over the next few years, they receive automated catalogs and helpful niche information. Every month I write a fresh newsletter and send it out. The newsletters have links to my website, books, products, blogs, and social network locations.

As with blogs, take an opportunity to earn residual income with advertising. You can reach out to like-minded businesses and offer them advertising space in your newsletter.

I mentioned that I did use an online newsletter service (www. icontact.com) to manage deliveries. You can schedule your deliveries for any time of the day. I prepare my newsletters over the weekend and schedule them for delivery on Tuesday mornings at 9:30 am. It's automated and I get a notification once complete.

Once I participated in a security conference. The gentleman in front of me suddenly looked down at his phone, then turned around and gave me a "what just happened" look. Later, he approached me and asked, "How did you send your newsletter while you were here?" That's why I love the automated system. Another positive is the sales spike within the following few days.

Website

Websites are a great way for people to find you. Your website should be intended to capture sales. Once people visit, they should be prompted to buy something or leave contact information. People who discover your site for the first time should learn to trust you as both a supplier and an expert in the field. Before they leave your web page, they have received information about your blogs and social networks, read your articles, and know that you are the one source provider of the niche products. In other words, though your website is the place customers decide to buy, it is also an information pipeline that they shouldn't be able to live without.

Online Articles

Ezinearticles.com is an online magazine and repository of articles written and filed by category. This offers an amazing marketing opportunity that costs absolutely nothing. The more articles you write the more sources for people to find you and your problem solving products. One such source is *ezinearticles.com*. They create metrics that follow the progress of articles. You can determine the effectiveness of your articles and see how many people read and forward them. You can also see how many readers followed the link to your website.

Additionally, *ezinearticles.com* sends a report to let you know how many times your most popular articles were read. They even help determine how to title your articles to attract more readers.

Without a goal and a direction, your marketing won't be effective. This focus begins with your profile. Make sure that your profile entry is up to date and indicates who you are, your purpose, business, and contact information. People who find your articles may want to know what makes you the expert. So, let them know.

Milestones

This site provides article data with the name, how many times the article was viewed, the amount of times your website link was clicked, what other websites and blogs featured the article, and how many times a reader emailed it to others.

If your article warranted comments, you can see how your audience responded. Readers can also rate your articles. You can perform more in depth article performance research by rearranging how you read the data. If you want to sort your articles by how many views, URL Clicks, Click Rate, EzinePublisher, Emailed, Comments, Votes or Rating, just select the appropriate header and your articles will be resorted.

Some data on the spreadsheet have hyperlinks that reveal more information. You can sort your articles by number of readings. Once sorted, you can select the number revealed to see further statistics about who viewed the articles. You can research the number of views by month as well as determine keyword searches that led readers to the article. The keyword terms are also provided by date. This is noteworthy, as you can always go back to add the same keywords to your website, blog, *Amazon.com* and other web based product listings. These keyword terms can help you get to the top of specific search engine results.

The data available can also reveal how many times people clicked on your website and which websites they visited. For example, if your articles are about bowling and you provide bowling resources, you can see if your articles lead readers to visit your website. Now, imagine you have several websites related to bowling. You might refer article readers to a blog of your experience, a website featuring your book, or another site where you feature self-designed bowling shirts. The "URL Clicks" column can tell you how many times readers visited and which websites they visited as led by each article. This provides valuable information on how well your articles work to generate visits to your website. These may then further develop into sales.

You can also view how many times your article was forwarded or posted on other websites. Though the information doesn't show where articles are posted or to whom they were emailed, they do demonstrate interest level. If someone thought enough of your article to forward it to a colleague or repost it on their blogs, you know there is interest. You can see how many people visited your article, but you can't be sure if they read it. But forwarding, that's a good news story. You can find out where your articles are posted by going to Google and typing in the article name in the search box. You can even do further market research on the article publisher's organization. For example, if an article you wrote is forwarded and posted on someone else's blog, you get more exposure. It may open up opportunities in your marketing footprint. Comment on your article at those sites and interact with their audience.

Votes and comments also count. Find out what kind of confidence people have in your articles as well as how they perceive you as an expert. Learn all you can about your articles through the clever article report system.

Become viral

These days, it's easier to become viral. Your blogs and online articles now provide the ability to create banners, widgets, and buttons that you can put on your website, blogs, and social networking engines. These are attractive and fit in well with your sites. One widget allows your articles to embed on your website. When readers visit your website, they get a free gift of reading your articles. You can also create a button that lets everyone know your status as an author. These techniques just help build your reputation as an expert.

Link your articles to email, websites, blogs, social networks, and etcetera. You can even publish your posts and articles on any social media sites you maybe be involved with.

Social Media

One day after a professional organization luncheon, I was stopped by a colleague. She told me that she had been searching for security information. She stated several times that her keyword searches brought her to my blogs and articles. This then led her to my websites. Talk about success, I was able to help her and build awareness of Red Bike Publishing at the same time. I also know that she is discussing me in professional circles. This will keep the buzz up and didn't cost me anything. I also use the same articles in blogs, newsletters, and other publications; a lot of impact with a little time investment.

You can also create a signature block or author resource box that appears at the end of your articles. Develop an overarching signature block to go with all of your articles, or customize several different author resource boxes to fit your various needs. My author profile or bio exists to support my niche expertise.

But what about my writing and publishing ventures? The next logical step is to add to my bio and add an additional customized author resource box to address each of my publishing efforts. The bio and resource boxes will reflect security expertise and the other, publishing and writing.

LinkedIn

LinkedIn has been a great networking opportunity. Those who have built great profiles have been offered jobs, writing opportunities, and more. LinkedIn has proven a very effective way for me to market books, again, without using paid advertising. I can demonstrate that group membership and contacts with members in my niche market have resulted in actual sales. I've joined and created many groups related to security, exporting, and publishing. I made specific and relevant comments, status updates, and information to my connections and groups that I've created and joined.

It may turn out that there are many in your niche that may not be actively engaged in social networking sites. This just creates awesome opportunities to be the first to jump in and be a subject matter expert. After you establish an account, you can create groups and invite like-minded people to join.

People can connect with you and follow your posts and updates. When you post information, it will automatically show up on the pages of those who are linked with you. These notifications will show up on the news feeds of everyone you are linked with.

There are other creative ways to send information to those you are linked with. LinkedIn allows you to send out polls, announcements, and other marketing opportunities to those in your network for free. If you want to get information to people outside of your network, it will cost you. If your niche market is large enough, it may be worth the cost. Otherwise, take advantage of the free things.

Do everything you can to contribute to others' successes and acknowledge their achievements. When you see those you are connected with achieve something, comment publicly. Let them know that you appreciate their accomplishments. Thank others publicly as well. If you had a good working relationship, provide a recommendation. This will allow others to build their credibility and provide a testimony of their excellent performance.

The good thing is that every time you write something on LinkedIn, there is a record. Your comments, recommendations, and other public remarks are posted for everyone to see. When you write about someone else, it is posted to all in your network as well as in the networks of others who you are complimenting. Also, don't be afraid to ask for recommendations from others. Recommendations appear prominently on your profile page.

Groups

You can perform a search for groups or individuals that have similar characteristics or interests. After you register and build your profile, start your search. In the upper right corner of the LinkedIn page is a search bar. Just select "People" or "Group" from the drop menu and type in keywords relevant to your niche. The search engine will find groups or persons with similar characteristics. Additionally, after you create your profile, LinkedIn will create hyperlinks to some of the words you use to set up your account. For example, under "Other Interests," you might list clubs, groups, hobbies, or organizations. LinkedIn will notify you of others who share the same interests, past employment, and job titles. You can select those links and discover potential connections and future customers.

If your search reveals people who work and operate in your niche, request to connect with them. If groups you are interested in already exist, request to join them. Once you become a member, the group's icon will show up on your profile. Spend some time researching members, discussion topics, news, and other group activities to see what they are interested in. You can also follow discussions and get a good idea of what is lacking in their field.

A good way to build trust within a group is to provide relevant comments to group discussions. When you become active in discussions, people will want to learn about you. They can click on your information and discover your books and products. You can take advantage of your membership to invite other members to be your contacts.

When you join a group, follow the rules. Try not to hijack the purpose of the group to meet your own goals. Believe it or not, you don't always have to be "on" as a sales person. Sometimes your sage advice and expertise as you reply to messages or provide news is enough. When people begin to respect your opinion, they'll ask more of you. I have been contacted many times by group members for advice and information. That's always free.

However, if you go in selling your product in inappropriate situations, you'll find yourself getting shunned, talked about by the group, or kicked out of the group. If you create good discussion, LinkedIn gives you credit by posting your picture and profile under the heading of "Top Influencers this Week."

Create groups

If you can't find groups or persons within your niche, then create your own. I've created groups, and each attracts my target market. I've even used my book covers as appropriate for the group's picture. As a result, I've had people join from outside organizations. I provide a great forum for discussions and incredible awareness of my products and profile; not just locally, but nationally.

Once you create a group, you can send out invitations to connect with fellow members. You can search for people using keywords that match your business profile, then send invitations to those who would likely fit in with the group. If you create a group, be sure to create criteria to enable you to be selective of who you allow to join. Many don't fit the profile of the group and are just joining as many groups as possible to sell their product. Protect your members or they will leave your group.

Once you create a group, you can invite others to join. They don't have to belong to LinkedIn for you to invite them. You can send an invitation to people in your email account. Click on "Manage." Once the Manage page opens, click the "Send Invitation" on the left side of the page. You can also invite LinkedIn Contacts and members of other LinkedIn groups. Send general messages by sharing your status on the Home page.

After you join or create a group, post messages by selecting the group's "discussion" tab and then select "start a discussion" once the page opens. The message format starts with a title. This is limited to a short title. Make it snappy enough to draw the desired result. "How do you____" or "What is the best way to _____" types of questions draw good responses. A controversial, but respectful, statement may provide more responses. One of the popular questions in one of my group discussions is "Why don't self-publishers just get out of the way and let real publishers take over?" elicited thousands of comments.

LinkedIn is an incredible way to network and direct customers to your point of sale. Be sure to use all the tools and applications available to invite other people to your profile and groups. Also, invite people from your email accounts to find your LinkedIn presence.

Facebook

Many claim that just because there are millions of people on Facebook, it pays to advertise. In reality, for niche businesses with a limited group of customers, only a small percentage of Facebook members will be impacted by your product. Unless you are selling to meet basic human needs, don't fall for the hype. Facebook is a social network with the emphasis on "social." It is not designed as a point of sale.

Facebook Page

Facebook does provide another avenue for branding and word of mouth. Once you have a personal account, you can create a Facebook page for your business. I created a page for my company, each of my books, and a group that hosts a professional certification.

Did you know that you can log into your individual pages and use make comments and "like" other comments as that entity?

Here's an example: I have a Facebook page called 80s Movie Reviews. To generate interest with other people who enjoy the 80s genre, I searched Facebook with the keywords: "80's, 80s, 80s music", and so on. Once I find those pages I make comments on their wall and "like" them using my 80s Movie Reviews profile.

This technique has increased visitors to my blog and Facebook pages by 200%. Imagine what it can do for your book, product, or fun trivia page. Hopefully, it will feed the publicity mill and give your pages the attention they deserve. Don't forget to include a link or call to action for potential customers to buy your products.

Info

 Start by adding your business information. Your potential audience will better understand what your books and products are about. Be sure to list all of your websites, including blogs and social networks. The page is not a point of sale, but your links can lead potential customers to find your books. Building your image and marketing your product on limited time is not hard. So, be sure to fill out your company overview, mission, and products with the same information as you used on all of your other social networks, websites, and blogs.

Photos

Use thumbnail photos of your book covers everywhere. Select the "Photos" tab and upload your page's profile photo. This might be a book or your business logo. Next, you can create an album featuring all of your books. Be sure to include a description about your books and products, as well as a place where customers can go to find more information and make a purchase. All of my book cover photos link to their *Amazon.com* book pages.

Be Creative

There are many more tabs allowing you to create discussions, blogs, and videos about your books and products. There are also a lot of ways to waste valuable time, so stay focused. Create the most professional and succinct page as possible, invite everyone you know to "like" your pages and post relevant information.

Your individual page should reflect your business as well. Make sure your posts and comments are clean, ethical and business related since you are, in essence, mixing your personal experience with your professional experience. Remain clean, sober, and polite while making comments. Avoid political and religious comments unless your page is politically and religiously oriented. You are free to express your beliefs on personal time, but it may hurt your professional image. Remember, what you put in Facebook can be accessed by anyone in your network. If you offend personal relationships, you might also offend those you are trying to do business with and vice versa.

You can also create a Facebook group and invite your contacts from your other social media. Groups are also more of a social function, reflecting the original mission of Facebook. Your posting to groups, in turn, supports your role as a recognized expert. When your group gets exposure, your business gets exposure. Look for similar groups, and invite them to join yours as you join theirs.

Facebook activity may not create sales, but it does extend your business footprint. Your individual account, group, or business page can point people to your product, as well as where to buy your product. Be sure to use all available tools and applications to announce your presence and invite others to join you. Facebook also provides ways to invite your email contacts to your Facebook presence.

Create Marketing Videos

I've seen some great video ideas and I am joining the many who post videos about their books or companies. So far, I've really enjoyed the fun and adventurous videos I've created that feature an idea and not books. These videos include Zombie vs. Ranger and How Not to Get a Consulting Job. These videos are meant to be fun and entertaining and don't even mention my products until the end.

However, I still can't discount the effectiveness of a good video featuring a specific product or book. Great graphics and the right type of music can combine to create a compelling reason for a viewer to take action. This action could include buying a product, visiting a website, or signing up for a newsletter.

Whatever call to action you want from your video, be sure to make the video worthy of watching. Here are five great tips for making a video trailer:

1. Invest in video software. There is great software that turns your pictures and videos into well organized, packaged, and presented products. They also offer free versions. However, I recommend investing some money on the entire package. You can get a good one for under $60. The free versions only allow a minute of video, hardly enough time to get the job done.

A good video package will allow you to perform graphic tricks like zooming, create text right in the video, highlight important parts, add soundtrack or voice over, and package the video for presentation in many formats. It's all simple to do without having to invest in training. You can learn it as you go.

2. Download great pictures for your video. A video doesn't always mean you will have motion. Sometimes it's composed of a collage of images. I recommend creating an account with *Istockphoto.com* and buying high definition photos. You can search images and videos

by subject and category. Find the ones you like and pay from $2 to download them.

3. Create a YouTube or Vimeo account. You will need a platform to host your videos. Once you create a video, upload it to the video account. From there, you can share it with the world. Make sure you create relevant keywords for search engines to find.

4. Post your videos on your website, newsletters, blog site, and social media locations. This is a great way to make your videos known to people who would not otherwise know about it. Don't wait for folks to use keywords to stumble across your video. That could take decades. Instead, take matters into your own hands and upload the videos to your sites.

Videos are a great way to showcase your work. They can be created in an hour or two, and can feature your product in many different venues.

Network Where Most Impactful

A good way to network is to attend seminars related to your book. Remember to bring plenty of pamphlets, business cards, postcards, free copies of books, and a way to close sales of any books or products. As an attendee, you can meet other professionals, network, and introduce yourself and your products. Though you don't have a display booth, you can just walk around introducing yourself and leave product information in highly visible areas.

Speaker/Vendor/Sponsor/Display

Whether or not to sign up as an event vendor depends on cost and probability of sales. The risk depends on how well your book relates to the event. In my case, I've sold books that help the attendees pass a security certification exam. The issue arises when comparing book sales with the cost of the display booth registration. In many seminars, vendors who set up booths to sell products and services earn thousands of dollars per contract. Booths are priced to get money from these clients. Unfortunately, book sales at those events won't generate that kind of revenue. Seminar officials don't usually prorate booths based on gross sales; it's one size fits all.

I have set up booths at smaller venues where costs were reasonable. I enjoyed the interaction with the audience, as well as the opportunity to make sales and collect data. If you decide to register as a vendor/ sponsor or display, keep in mind that the costs could go very high. Registration, travel, hotel, and other fees could make this a ridiculous proposition.

For example, I was invited to sell my books at a national seminar. The costs included: registration fee $3,000; round trip airfare $750; and hotel stay $200 per night. There are other expenses, but we can just stop here in the example. From studies that I have conducted, I learned that I can expect up to ten percent of attendees to buy my books. I can have sixty books available at the publisher cost of $407 (printing plus shipping and handling). For $4357 I could set up a booth and have my books exposed to a target audience of 600 people.

The Math. Suppose I sell all 60 books for $45 each. That would add up to $2,700.

$4357-$2700=$1657 loss

At this particular event, vendors receive a copy of attendees' contact information; that's gold. Suppose I used an email campaign to send further information. From studies I've seen, only 1% of these make a buying decision. That's six more books; not quite enough to make up the difference. Of course, you could argue that that's the price of marketing. You might be right. However, there are so many more free and inexpensive ways to make sales.

Though I turned down that offer, I did accept an offer to be a vendor at a smaller venue of the same organization. Their costs were only $250 for the booth space and there were 400 people in attendance. I sold enough books and made a small profit. I also built great credibility with colleagues and fellow professionals. That event worked out well for me. I also received a mailing list which I continue to use to this day. So, if the price is right, you can get time off from your day job, and you have the sales potential, go for it.

If you do decide to set up a booth, do so with the intent to accomplish two things:

1. Have a point of sale, and

2. Collect information for future points of sale

Work outside the booth

I've been amazed at how little some vendors work toward these two goals. They pay good money to display their wares, but do not interact very well with potential customers. They stand at their booths and hand out swag (free stuff) containing their contact information. Not surprisingly, they do little to collect customer data. I've seen authors do the same at book signings. Always have a plan to collect information and make sales.

I don't recommend giving away free stuff unless they are articles or strategically placed free books. Providing pens, calendars, and other promotional items is just too expensive and doesn't generate sales. However, you can do something much more effective that will actually measure success and lead to clients swarming to your booth while not paying any attention to the other vendors.

Go prepared to sell. Have inventory on hand and a way to collect money. Cash always works; accept checks at your own risk and use a credit card machine at your own expense.

Because the professional organization happens to be corporate security professionals, I do accept checks and sometimes I even provide a way to invoice through PayPal. I allow the customer to take the products after I collect Name, Company, Email, Phone Number and Address information. Later, I send an invoice to the address and the money comes either by corporate check or through PayPal. I've always received payment. However, you may not have such a convenience. If not, consider another way to collect money or do the following:

1. Give out fliers and business cards to everyone you meet. Give them an option to visit your website or *Amazon.com* to find your book and make a purchase.

2. Have a drawing for free copies of your book. Design postcards or some way to collect registration information (collect Name, Company, Email, Phone Number and Address information).

3. Provide a way for clients to register for your newsletter. Again, collect the Name, Company, Email, Phone Number and Address information so that you can input it into your newsletter generator. It also gives permission for you to put them on your mailing list. The more potential customers are exposed to your books, the more chances you will have to close a sale. You can still collect the vital information and follow-up later with additional information about your products.

4. Visit other vendors, learn about their products, and see if you can work together. I've sold books to other vendors, registered them for my newsletters, given free book copies for publicity, and have sold advertising space. Other vendors are not your competition, they are opportunities.

Speaking Events

I often speak at security conferences as a subject matter expert. While there, I try to sell books and provide advice and assistance. If you are a niche expert, chances are that someone will also contact you to present, especially if you have a book, blog, or other product identifying you as the go-to person. In fact, you might receive a letter with wording similar to the one that I received.

"Dear __(fill in your name)___, we are contacting you to see if you are available to present at __(name of upcoming event)_____ conference. We thought it would be a good idea to present some information from your book _(your book title)_____.

Please let us know if you are available and how much you would charge as compensation…"

If this has happened to you, congratulations, you just made it to the big leagues. The two critical steps are to negotiate the payment and knock the ball out of the park with a grand slam presentation.

The last sentence "please let us know…how much you would charge for compensation" is the hardest to address. We all have an idea for payment in mind, but just like a job interview, we can really stumble answering this question, especially if it's your first time at bat.

1. There are several ways you can answer this question and it depends on your situation:

a. Will you travel to the event? Figure in ALL expenses.

b. Will you need to spend the night? Figure in sleeping and eating arrangements.

c. Will you have to take time off from your writing or full time job? Figure in these expenses, usually an hourly wage.

 The point is, you do not want to go broke on a business endeavor. You don't even want to break even. It's important for your expenses, convenience, and profit to be included in payment. However, there are trade-offs that can offset costs.

For example, I covered all bases with my last speaking engagement with a direct bill and some compromises.

My last speaking engagement required a 750 mile round trip and two overnights. Though I only spoke for an hour, I had to consider the logistics cost for travel and missing two days of work. Since I presented to a professional organization that supported government contracts, I asked for the equivalent of government per diem, lodging rates, and per mile driving reimbursement (what the government would spend to put up employees in a hotel, feed them, and pay per mile to get them there).

Wow, all expenses paid vacation to the beach! However, I still had to figure in the cost of being off the job for two days. You can do this by figuring how much you earn per hour and apply it to the amount of business hours you will be out of the office. You might even consider the cost of leaving your family behind and missing important events.

This is where I negotiated a value trade-off. I was able to get free booth space and permission to display and sell books at the event. Many organizations charge vendors anywhere from $300 to $3500 to occupy booth space. Though reasonable for a vendor with a $3,000 product, for a book seller, this is a lot of money. Where many vendors can earn a profit with the sale of one product or service, authors and book sellers would have to sell anywhere from ten to one hundred books to a potential audience of less than five hundred attendees; that defies the odds. In reality, you can expect to make a sale from 1-5% of attendees based on sales statistics. If you've read earlier chapters, you'll understand why I rarely ever pay for booth space.

So, the booth space and other compensation provided the win-win situation I looked for. Here are other ideas you can negotiate to cover expenses:

Ask organization to purchase a minimum number of books.
Ask for free advertising in upcoming newsletters or on their website.

Collect attendee names to include in your newsletter.

2.   Knock the presentation out of the park. This begins as soon as you accept terms. Now that you have their attention, get as much information on their playbook as you can and engage with the intended audience regularly.

a.   What is the theme of the seminar? You can ensure your presentation carries on not only the topic, but the setting. The conference I spoke at featured an Olympic theme. To support the theme, my presentation featured Olympic art and photos as well as how to be a "World Class Security Manager" while comparing the niche expert with an athlete in training.

b.   What will the others be presenting? A colleague contacted me as soon as he found out I was speaking. His main point was to let me know what he was presenting, so that I would not present the same information. In a small niche world, it's not out of the realm of possibility to present the same topic.

c.   Who will attend? This is important to determine the technical level of the folks you are presenting to. The last thing you want to present is something too far above or below their skill level. They pay good money to learn something new, so keep information fresh. Instead of offering the same old tired topic, how about presenting something they haven't seen before?

d.   Who are the other vendors? This is a good time to get to know the other vendors and make alliances. I've sold books and advertising space to other vendors. I made it my job to get to know them and go from rookie to MVP among vendors.

e.   Add all attendees or event POCs to newsletter. This not only allows you to introduce yourself, but ensures that everyone knows who you are prior to your arrival. Communicate continuously before, during, and after the event.

f.   Attend any social events planned. The organization that invited me to speak put up a world class social. Many members were invited. I had a great time meeting attendees and members the night before I presented. This both bolstered my confidence and gave me the opportunity to build my credibility as an expert.

If you are a niche expert, chances are that you'll be invited to teach or present at a seminar. If so, make sure you ask for proper compensation and prepare a presentation that knocks their socks off. Congratulations, you just made it to the big leagues, now prepare ahead of time to play well.

Sponsor a Professional Seminar

You can also sponsor niche related seminars as an advertiser or vendor. Many seminars require a sponsorship fee of several hundred to several thousand dollars. I have found that many will waive the fee in lieu of free books. I have sent anywhere from three to sixty books, depending on the size of the organization. Again, as publisher, the books were provided at only the cost of printing and shipping.

The payoff was Red Bike Publishing's name being branded as an official sponsor. I have received positive feedback, contact information of all attendees, and incredible sales after the fact. If you can't attend a seminar, sponsoring one can be just as effective.

At one seminar, an attendee ordered a copy of one of the books for each of their employees. This more than covered the cost of books I provided. I am also realizing big sales on the same book at *Amazon. com* and setting up "seller accounts" with book distributors and colleges.

In another example, I used contact information from a sponsored seminar and sent an email offering the recipients a complimentary subscription to my industry newsletter. I signed up many more attendees to my newsletter and catalog, all for the cost of eighty books.

This also led to $2000 in sales of one book. With an approximate cost of $400, it was not a bad investment.

Email campaign

Email campaigns are still a good way to reach potential customers. Email can be a low or no cost marketing endeavor provided you have a good mailing list and the time to put it together. Purchased mailing lists can cost thousands of dollars and they may not always hit your target market, especially in a specialized industry.

However, you can create pinpoint email campaigns to a small group of influential people. As a provider of security products, I had trouble finding my target audience. I, too, inquired of mailing list providers who did not understand my market. I also tried to put together my own email list, and after several attempts, I discovered an easier way.

I put together a mailing list by performing a Google search using keywords for email addresses. You can find your niche audience by searching for "chapter chair" or "chapter president" and use keywords of an organization related to your niche. For example, a safety professional might search for "chapter chair" and "safety," "OSHA," "industrial safety" or other applicable keywords for finding your related professional organizations.

If an organization exists, they can find an email or mailing address. I found similar opportunities and sent messages to local chapter chairpersons of a national professional organization in which I offered free books for door prizes. Though it wasn't a direct sell campaign, the email contact branded my company as a provider of books to the professional organizations. I sent the chairpersons free books for door prizes at their events, and forwarded copies of my email newsletters. The individual members of the organization gladly received free books and newsletter information. I realized an increase in sales and newsletter subscriptions. One organization stopped using their newsletter and continues to forward mine to all of their members.

Signature block

Use all of your contact information in your email signature block.
If you have a web, social network, blog, and other Internet presence,
list it in your email signature block. Associate your name with your
books, products, and website locations. When you send emails, curious
recipients will be able to discover what it is you might be up to. Be
everywhere all the time.

SUMMARY

Work your niche marketing with a purpose. There are plenty of
opportunities to do free marketing, publicity, and advertising if
you make a plan and stay committed. Social networks, websites,
newsletters, blogs, and meeting professionals with a purpose in mind
will help you get your message out and make real sales. Create a
marketing plan and use available resources to advertise free of charge.

CHAPTER 9 SPIN OFF

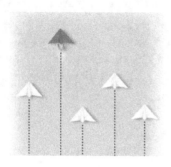

INTRODUCTION

Don't just stop at one book. Now that you've gained momentum, think of new and creative ways to help meet your customers' needs. You're working on the hardest part: to get people to trust you well enough to buy your book. Now that they are hooked, they are likely to continue shopping with you. As your online articles and social networking postings invite people to your website, your site further directs them how to buy books, register for your newsletter, and buy your niche related products.

It's not always easy to think of ways to meet customer needs, but I'll help you develop a method to discover openings or opportunities within your niche. You can maintain that creativity and continue to perpetuate your role as an expert and provider. As you write, publish, and market your book, you may become inspired to create related products. I'll use my own story and products in this chapter to explain new and creative ways to reach your market with viable products. Spin-off items could be additional books or closely related items or services.

Automate Your Sales

While preparing to go on vacation, I was concerned about how to handle my publishing and book selling business. Sure, I'm online and so are my book sales, but I will still have to advertise and fulfill sales while gone.

I can't afford to hang a sign on my website saying, "Gone fishing, be back in two weeks." I don't think potential customers would understand. I don't think you can afford to do so either. So, what is a niche publisher to do?

Use the tools available. The following are just a few tools that every niche publisher and author should have. They are affordable and will help returning customers build confidence in your products and services. First and foremost, make your primary point of sale at digital bookstores such as Barnes and Noble and *Amazon.com*. That way when customers buy, you are not in the middle of the sale. Once I set up titles, I don't have to do anything else. However, this is just the minimum. There are other options:

1. Use your business website to direct customers. You can feed your blogs and keep content fresh so that search engines will find your books. Customers can learn about your business, you as an author, and the books you write and sell. This is where they make their buying decision. Provide a link to where your books are available for sale, so customers can bring your books up with one click. However, maybe your customers prefer to buy directly from your website. If that's the case, look into the following options:

a. Add buying options on your website. Use a service like PayPal. PayPal has free shopping cart buttons that you can download and put on your site. You set the buttons' requirements with price, delivery, and other details. The customer buys and the order is fulfilled. This is effective for downloads or where automated shipping is available. It's completely automatic and, once set up, brings the person out of the loop.

b. Augment PayPal buttons with services like *Ejunkie.com*. This service allows me to upload digital books on a secure server. It also provides a service I haven't found with PayPal: customer options to add multiple products to shopping carts. *Ejunkie.com* takes care of orders, provides protected downloads of digital books, and sends reports.

2. Use a newsletter service such as *icontact.com* to keep your customers up to date. Before I leave on extended vacations, I program all my newsletters to send while I am gone. This ensures that customers remain up to date on product offerings and informative articles even when I'm not around. My newsletter also feeds to my social media accounts. That way, not only do subscribers get the newsletter, but so do my extended networks.

Spin-off Products

Synergy comes to mind describing what could happen next for the published author. The effort that goes with writing, marketing, and selling products combines for tremendous opportunity to help others and earn more income. Published authors are recognized as experts; recognition leads to conversation and comments; and conversation and comments lead to expressed needs. The expressed needs fill voids with potential products.

After publishing books, articles, blog posts, and teaching college courses and seminars, I reached my goal of becoming an expert two years early. Where I began in obscurity, people now ask for my opinion. It is an incredible and humbling experience. Additionally, I began to receive comments like: "We just don't have a resource for security container or open/closed magnets.," "Have you thought about index cards for some of your test questions?", "You might do well to have a class on how to prepare for the certification." and "I can't believe there isn't some type of college course." All of these are real comments from real customers who began to trust me as their provider. Not only were they able to use my products, but they wanted a source for other related products.

While others in my industry focus on consulting, I decided that I wanted to base my business on product lines that I could source single-handedly. After reading many business books, I agreed with the three partners (me, myself, and I) that I could run and manage a successful business by devoting time and energy writing once, designing once, and selling it multiple times. If I could just create something worthwhile, I could sell it over and over again. The idea of many spin-off products manifested and now continues to develop. The follow are some examples of spin-off ideas I created that may help you generate ideas.

Design Once

Take a look at books on your shelf. They are written, rewritten and finally published. Most fiction ends up on bookstore shelves for a few months. The more successful genre of nonfiction books continue to earn revenue for many years without major modification. Unless the book is ultra-trendy, the topic will continue to generate sales as long as the interest remains strong. I published my bestselling certification book in 2008 and it continues to gain momentum with new and veteran customers, and now the follow-up security books are well received. My business started out with one book, and now we have twenty books and multiple authors.

Why, because I've been writing and rewriting, the topic is still fresh and relevant and should be for years to come. There have been no changes in the industry requiring modifications or the introduction of new editions. You can have the same success with your books.

Security Container Magnets

My first spin-off product was a natural progression. I discovered that people needed a supplier for magnets to post on their security containers. By way of explanation, sensitive documents require storage in a security container (safe). In many cases, notifications are required on the safe to show that it is open or secure. This requirement creates a natural customer market. Some of the magnets are provided with the sale of a safe, but there weren't any resources for aftermarket versions. Many professionals resorted to creating them on personal printers with off the shelf label magnets from office supply stores. Others found suppliers who sold them for up to twenty dollars each. I recognized this as a significant consumer need that I could fill quickly, and many businesses have placed orders for hundreds of magnets.

The good thing about my business model is that I could build and operate debt free. It is a great feeling to make tons of money without contributing money up front. I performed Internet research to find vendors who made magnets. I communicated with several until I found possible solutions. All I needed to do was choose one.

I advertised my magnets on my webpage, newsletter and social networking system before even purchasing an inventory. My provider could make products available in plenty of time after placing my first order. This allowed me to test the market before I even created the product. My selected vendor could make my magnets for thirty-three cents each if I ordered five hundred.

 I advertised my magnets for four dollars each and began to receive orders within a week. I was able to realize a profit after just a few orders. My other magnets cost one dollar each for a minimum order of five hundred and I sold them for $6.95 each. Again, I realized a profit as soon as customers placed their orders, sometimes up to one hundred magnets at a time.

Certification Test Taking Tips

My next spin-off product was a failed freebie. Yes, that's right, a failed free product. I had a colleague make the comment that I should create and sell a study course based on my certification book. I didn't think that it would sell, so I created a free presentation on how to study for the ISP Certification. However, I didn't get any takers.

Let me give some history. In the beginning, I priced my certification book at eighteen dollars. I didn't realize great sales until I increased the price.

After doing market research and comparing with similar books, I reset the price at sixty dollars before realizing significant sales. Point of sale and price are critical to success. Sometimes a high price tag increases perceived value with customers.

I applied the same logic to the failed freebie presentation. The value of the presentation is it prepares people to take the exam. Sample questions, word search methods, and study aids help students become more informed about the exam. However, my audience realized no value in a free product. I finally began listing it starting at five dollars and raising it to its current price before sales took off.

This product is a PowerPoint presentation converted to Adobe PDF. I've also used it to provide live study events for our professional organization meetings. It took minimal extra time or creativity since I had already written the material for classes and the book. I created it once and use it in multiple applications; the perfect business formula.

The presentation has sold well and I enjoy knowing that I am helping people pass the exam. I included the prerequisites that professionals need to meet and how to sign up for the certification exam. I also included a breakdown of the organization of the open book exam and methods to use to search for the correct answers. Also included are three test-taking methods for finding answers in the open book exam.

Feedback

As my newsletter audience grew, I began to receive more feedback from my customers. I'm proud of the contact that I've made with my customers and I am always happy to receive feedback.

Flash Cards

"Why don't you make flashcards?" A customer asked. He further explained that flashcards were a unique way for people to study. I agreed with him and immediately contacted a local printer. They quoted a good price for one hundred cards front and back. These cards are large and the size of a quarter sheet of 8.5 in. x 11 in. paper. This is a standard size for printers to cut and since it equally divides this size paper, it is much cheaper to make than smaller sizes normally used for flash cards. I used a Word document in the landscape orientation. I then divided the page into four sections. On the front side I copied and pasted practice questions from my book and on the reverse I copied and pasted the answers. It worked great.

I also found a supplier for large index card cases. This supplier sells the cases in various colors. The cases hold the one hundred cards easily and have a little window in the front just the right size for a business card. I also include a business post card and other product information. The entire package fits well inside of a small flat rate US Postal Service Priority Mail box. I am able to receive triple the price of printing the cards including the nice storage box, while still providing the excellent value added for my customers. I have not been able to automate this system yet, but also continue to enjoy interaction with my customers as PayPal notifies me of the sale and provides customer information.

This product has also evolved into two more flashcard ideas: eFlash cards and an online practice exam. So, from one book, I've been able to generate additional products to help my customers.

Training Resources

The National Industrial Security Program Operating Manual (NISPOM) is the rule book that governs how defense contractors protect government information. Since it is the playbook, businesses falling under the NISPOM have training and performance measures they are inspected against. This provides an excellent resource for designing and providing training to security managers and their employees.

I have taken chapters from the NISPOM and designed appropriate, applicable, and easy to understand self-paced classes. The customers download training directly to their computers. They can either teach the presentations to their employees or provide them to their employees for self-study. The training is complete with notes for the instructor to use while presenting mandatory training topics. Customers are also able to tailor the training to fit unique contract driven requirements. This provides a win-win situation for both my business and the customer.

More Books

If you have published your first book, you now have the experience to publish more. If new books are within the same genre or specialized area, great for you. That just means that your first customers just might be repeat customers. If you can come up with additional books or products relative to the needs of your current audience, then you may have guaranteed future success. Additionally, customers who come to know your business through current marketing efforts will buy all of your book and product selections.

Some may not view an eBook as a spin-off product, but it is a viable product that you should consider. I began selling my manual as an eBook. Since the certification exam offers an online testing option, I planned on customers buying the book and practicing taking the test online. I created the book using Microsoft Word and converting it to Adobe Acrobat. It was a good product that customers could buy directly from me. I had originally sold it on eBay and my website. Sales were slow, but soon picked up enough to gain my full attention.

I finally matured the process and developed a printed book. Soon, sales really took off. Simultaneously, I focused on refining the eBook into a professional product. I used Ingram Content Group to publish it with online stores that specialize in eBooks.

Since the item is sold in Internet bookstores, I don't have to take orders or prepare them for shipment. I just read reports provided by Ingram Content Group and collect revenue in my bank account. Sales of this product are still slower than the paperback, but supplement my business income. While publishing eBooks, consider all format alternatives. Not every eBook reader can read all eBooks. Some read only Adobe PDF or product unique proprietary software. Consider multiple eBook venues such as Amazon's Kindle and Barnes and Noble's Nook.

My second spin-off book is a pocket edition of the certification book. This is a smaller edition in every sense of the word. Where the original is 8.5 in. x 11in., this second book is 9 in. x 5 in. It is more compact and looks more like a standard book size. This book took much less time to write and design as it is exactly the same in every instance as the original. The only difference is that it contains half of the material as the first book. Instead of 440 questions in four separate practice exams, it only has 220 questions in two practice exams. I also kept the cover design the same and added Pocket Edition-1 as part of the title.

Keep in mind that just because much of the material is the same, it is a completely new book and has a new ISBN. If you are self-publishing and using Ingram Content Group, you've already got an account and adding additional books is just a repeated process.

The marketing part is easier with the online bookstores. Because it has a new ISBN, the second book is listed as a separate book in bookstores. However, the great thing is that both books are related and often linked by relationship, author profile, and book topic. When this happens on *Amazon.com*, the book page will feature all related books listed under "What others have bought after viewing this book."

I have another opportunity for a similar spin-off book. Now I can have a second pocket edition using the second half of the test. All I need to do is develop the front matter, and provide the remaining two practice tests for the title *Pocket Edition-Version 2*. Do you see possibilities to spin-off books from the book you are working on now? With just a little effort, you may be able to publish or write several books simultaneously.

I can also print related public domain government regulations. Since many are in the public domain, they are not owned by a copyright. However, you can put them in a book format and copyright your original material such as the cover or front matter. If you have experience with government regulations, you may have noticed that many are already formatted in Microsoft Word or Adobe PDF. Professionals who are governed by policy refer to the regulations often. The Government Printing Office does not provide hard copies as they used to. Now, we have an opportunity to assist new customers. Otherwise, if someone wants a copy of a government publication, they have to print them on their desk side or company printer. Often, it is expensive and the print quality is poor.

Items in the Public Domain

For those of you who have decided to form your own publishing company, the following provides a unique opportunity. You can print regulations and sell them to customers. In my case, I have printed several government and industry regulations. Customers who bought my first book also bought the associated regulations. Additionally, people who have searched for and found the regulations have bought my first book. By publishing same niche book topics, I have increased sales many times over.

I provide these professionally printed books and save customers the hassle of printing them on a desk side printer and carrying them around in three ring binders or comb bound volumes. The new policy of going green has created a golden opportunity. People still want something printed. Printing on desk side printers does no one any favors. The print quality is bad, and eventually comb bound, three-hole punch, and stapled document pages fall out.

Since most government documents already have a table of contents and format that the readers are intimately familiar with, I don't usually change a thing. I just download the Adobe PDF document and insert my own front and back matter. If I do need to create a table of contents, index, or additions to the original document, I do so with Microsoft Word as described earlier.

You will need to create additional book matter before publishing. The book title, copyright, ISBN, and publisher information pages are still necessary. We'll call this the "front matter." The public domain material will be called the "main document." The last page should be a list of your books and products called the "back matter." Save the front and back matter as separate files and convert them to Adobe PDF using Adobe Professional. Don't forget to format them using the correct page sizes.

CREATING YOUR PRODUCTS

I shared my success story to teach you what I have learned in my adventure to become a niche expert and self-publisher. I've read a lot of books on writing, publishing and marketing and all have been excellent references. However, they were not written for a niche publisher/author. While I could not have gotten where I am without reading these great helps, I feel there is more that I can teach you. Specifically, not all writing, publishing, and marketing efforts will work every time and within every niche.

What this means for you is a streamlined approach to creating and selling your books and spin-off products. One thing that I have to my advantage is professional organization and federal guidelines for the national security industry. These provided the blueprint for many of my ideas. Just by anticipating new requirements and discovering some needs, I can create new products. As a vendor or supplier, I can use my core competencies as a publisher, consultant, teacher, and author to provide products that businesses cannot make themselves. Because of what I do, customers are able to access new products and services. With this book, I can help entrepreneurs, niche experts, and self-publishers get information out faster.

Your Resources

Does your specialized market have written guidance or requirements such as state or federal regulations, policy, or procedures or any other publication of rules? If so, read all you can to understand more in depth. You might have a good opportunity to reach more of your target market. In my experience, people seem to work under best practices and not necessarily regulatory guidance. This opens up even more opportunities for products.

Another place to search for implied spin-off products is a niche organization's website, newsletter, blog, or other publication. Maybe your niche area is a hobby and has nothing to do with regulation. However, organizational or hobby by-laws, newsletters, or other publications may exist with information for valuable spin-off ideas. Articles and other writings may give clues to myriad unmet needs. Spin-off ideas may come quickly, so be sure to take notes (Figure 9-1).

I've created an exercise template for you to use (Figure 9-2). The following are some suggested spin-off books related to my niche industries. Your specialty area isn't featured, but you can use the information to help you determine what you can do in your specialized field. An electronic version is available at:

www.redbikepublishing.com/nicheworkbook

HOME OFFICE OPERATIONS

Find supplier

You can find suppliers on the Internet for almost every need. Use Google or your favorite search engine to find resources. Search for a vendor who provides resources to a broad customer base. You'll design the product specifically for your niche base. Remember that you are creating a product to sell and not a publicity gimmick or marketing campaign. For example, I use a vendor to make magnets for customers to buy and not for marketing or branding purposes.

Niche Market Spin-off Idea #1
For Publication: ISP Certification-The Industrial Security Professional Exam Manual
Idea: Security Container Magnets
Reason: Security Professionals Use Industrial Security Program Operating Manual as study source. This regulation governs how security managers implement security programs. Security containers are a part of their working environment. Magnets are applied to each security container.
Strong selling point 1: There is no source for magnets on the Internet. The security containers are sold with magnets; however after market varieties are not available.
Strong selling point 2: Because of strong selling point number 1, security managers create their own magnets using desk side printers, downloaded software and printable magnets available at office supply stores. This results in low quality printing and flimsy magnets.
Strong selling point 3: Continue as needed
Strong selling point 4: Continue as needed
Strong selling point 5: Continue as needed
Figure 9-1 Spin Off Idea Worksheet

To find a supplier, enter keywords for your intended product into the search menu. For example, to find someone to make magnets, I enter, "magnet, signs, two sided magnet." After selecting search, you will find many providers. Compare their products and select a few who you think may be able to provide items that your customers might want.

Take a look at ordering in volume; the more you order, the cheaper you may be able to acquire them. Before you place a large order, test the market by offering the product on your website, blogs, newsletters, and social networks. Don't forget to associate a ton of keywords related to your product so potential customers can land on your website. Whatever you use to make your website, insert the keywords everywhere in your product description.

As people begin to find your page, they'll start placing orders. If you don't have inventory on hand, be sure to let the potential customer know that it may take two weeks to fill an order. Once you get your first order, contact your supplier and order the inventory.

Niche Title	Published Book Title	Regulations or Guidelines?	Spin-off Product 1	Spin-off Product 2	Spin-off Product 3	Spin-off Product 4
ISP Certification	ISP Certification-The Industrial Security Professional Exam Manual	National Industrial Security Operating Manual (NISPOM)	Magnets	Study Tips	Flash-cards	Security Training

Figure 9-2 Spin Off Template

MAKING PRODUCTS AVAILABLE

Make ordering as easy as possible for your customers. I put links
to Amazon for customers to purchase the books. This provides a
seamless process that doesn't require my involvement as it's a "hands
off" system. The more books that sell, the better the statistics and
chances for reviews. Statistics and reviews increase book sales. If I had
a preference, I would have everyone order from Amazon as it would
perpetuate my future sales.

I also provide a point of sale on my website using PayPal. I collect
buyer information and create opportunities to sell combinations
of books at a reduced rate. I end up selling more books because of
Amazon.com, but offer PayPal as a method of payment if customers
do not or cannot order through *Amazon.com*. You can experiment
by selling your books on your website with other spin-off products.
Consider the option of offering bundles of combined products with
customers receiving discounts for multiple or large orders.

Collecting Payment

There are a lot of options available for payment accounts, so do some
research for the best bargain. I use PayPal because there are no upfront
costs for set up. PayPal takes a percentage of the customer's payment.
If sales are $3,000 or less, PayPal will charge a percentage of sales plus
a small amount per transaction. If your sales are in the higher range, it
might be worth looking into another vendor's products.

PayPal Options

PayPal provides great options for receiving payments. If you sell
products directly from your website, PayPal provides the payment
buttons "Buy Now" and "Shopping Cart." These track payments and
guide the customer through the payment process. As seller, you can
customize necessary additional fees and taxes. For example, you can
require shipping fees based on price or weight.

Create a PayPal Account

Just follow the instructions for creating an account and you are in business. After you create your account, go to the "Merchant Services" tab and begin by setting up your PayPal button. You can create your own or use PayPal's design. Once you select the create button link, your first option is to decide which type to make. I'll walk you through customizing a "Buy Now" button if you are not familiar with the process.

Create a Button

Step one is to choose the button type. I like to use the "Add to Cart" button. This allows customers to add several items. If you just have one product, you can choose a "Buy Now" button. The "Buy Now" button doesn't allow for more than one purchase at a time. Next, give your product a name. Choose a name that you will recognize when the customer makes a purchase. This will eliminate confusion if you have multiple products. Be careful to clearly distinguish similar products so that when orders come you will have a clear understanding of what the customer ordered. For example, I have two types of magnets for sale. One is an OPEN/CLOSED two sided magnet and the other is a magnet that looks like a telephone touch pad. I will name one magnet "OPEN/CLOSED" and the other "Telephone." If I use "Magnet" as the title, it might lead to product confusion and I end up mixing up orders. Keep the title simple but clear.

Next, select the price in the currency you wish to collect. You can select multiple price options by leaving this item blank. For example, I might create different sizes of similar magnets at different prices. I can create a button with a drop down menu to make pricing similar. Or, I can just create separate buttons with different prices by size.

Shipping Methods

If you charge shipping and handling, you can put that in the shipping option. You can specify your shipment charges here, or do as I have done and create shipping specifications in your profile. To do so, go to the "My Account" tab and select the "My Profile" option. On the right hand column are options for many selling preferences to include shipping and tax options. For shipping fees, select "Shipping Calculations."

Select "Add Shipping Method." This will open a new window where you can select the shipping destination. It can be by state or select "All States and Territories." Next, you can select a shipping method. I prefer to send Priority Mail. You can select delivery duration, and whether to charge by weight, cost, or quantity. I have "select cost" as my option and have listed the cost of shipment with ranges. It is important that you are able to recover shipping costs.

Next, decide on your ship from address. It can be the address in your account profile or something different. You can select the carrier if you have a preference between United States Postal Service and United Parcel Service.

The next option is how you want to be notified of account activity. When a customer makes a purchase, or whenever you make a transaction, PayPal sends an email. The option is whether you want all email sent to the email address you created in your account, or another one that you'd like to enter.

Next, track inventory. This allows you to control your inventory should you have a limited supply. You can save your created buttons for later, have PayPal track and report low inventory, and product profit and loss information.

You can control customer activity and decide whether or not customers can change their order quantities. If you select yes, they may add more to the order. By selecting no, you give them no opportunity to change their mind unless they cancel out the order and start over.

The next option is to decide whether or not to allow the customer to leave instructions or comments. If you select yes, the customer will be given the option of typing in a field and the message will go to your email. I allow customers to send instructions. It is a great opportunity to interact with the customer, as well as ensure that I fill the order correctly.

The next selection allows you to decide whether or not you need a shipping address. Whether or not you are shipping out items or providing automatic downloads, always collect customer information for newsletters, product catalogs, or any other customer contact need.

The final options allow you to direct the customer to your webpages if they choose to cancel or complete an order. Always direct them to your website with a "thank you for your order" page or a message notifying them of an order cancellation. Include options to buy more products and join your newsletter. After customers complete a transaction, they are directed to my website and a message appears, "Congratulations on your purchase and thanks for visiting Red Bike Publishing. We are preparing your order for shipment and will get it to you immediately. Consider joining our newsletter and keeping up with the latest in the industrial security profession."

Experiment with the "My Profile" menu and learn all you can about PayPal if you decide to use their services. I've given you the basics here, but there are many more options which I cannot possibly include in this book.

Invoicing

PayPal can help you create invoices. Under PayPal's "Merchant Services" tab, you can select and create customized invoices. After setting up the invoice, PayPal will enable you to send an original and reminder emails to customers for payment. Once sent, the emails allow your customer to pay via PayPal, credit card, check or any other offline option you can think of. I send books and products to clients who do not wish to order online and follow-up with invoicing. This helps me build trust and continue to meet client needs.

On those rare occasions where I've set up booths at conferences, I've provided invoices for customers who did not have cash. I did not have a credit card collection process away from my computer. Customers visiting my website may request alternate payment. In those cases, I create invoices using PayPal. You can find invoices under the Merchant Services tab. On the left side under the heading "Manage Payments" is the "Send Invoice" option.

This will open a new window. The first screen features a drop down menu where you can create a new invoice or open a saved invoice. Select "New Invoice" and a new window appears where you can complete a form. When finished, you can save it and email it to your customer. The customer receives it and makes payment. The Invoicing allows you to create, name, and save an invoice for your products. You can pull up and reuse old invoices.

Subscription

You can also use PayPal to create subscription opportunities for advertisers, newsletters, training events, or whatever you desire. PayPal will automatically keep track of the payment dates and send reminders to your customers. Customers who have selected the subscription can unsubscribe at any time.

The only problem I've encountered with PayPal is that many new customers don't understand how to use it. They assume they must have a PayPal account to make a purchase. It is in your best interest to explain that PayPal allows credit card payment. I've received several phone calls from customers who don't understand the process and I've had to walk them through it. Be careful to keep instructions short and precise. You don't want the customers to become distracted from the purchase by reading too much. Simply write "We accept all major credit cards. Please select the Pay Now button and follow the link to credit card payment."

Protect Your Product

While Internet marketing offers great options for publishers to promote their books, ethical and legal lines can seem blurred. This is especially true for posted images and materials and how they are actually used. As an author, publisher, marketer, or other web entrepreneur, you have access to several free metric sources to track your products' sales performance and clue you into where and how to market.

Google Analytics, *Blogger.com* and other resources can help you track your books' online presence and include information such as who is viewing, where they are viewing from, what they viewed, how long they viewed, and how they got there. It can also give insight into how many page views it takes before someone makes a purchase.

However, there is not much available (that I'm aware of) by way of technology to track the use of your proprietary information or intellectual data. Most of that stuff is protected by existing laws such as the ones governing copyrights and trademarks. Here are some examples of problems you could face:

1. Blogs and newsletter articles are stolen and attributed to someone else. I've had entire articles of an extremely niche nature stolen, published word for word on another blog, and attributed to an entirely different author or included in a book, magazine, or other publication.

2. Books and covers are copyrighted. However, book covers and graphics can also be stolen and used. There are many opportunities to lift images of search results for use on websites, magazines, and other media.

Here are some ways you can discover how your work is being used:

Frequently search for your book titles, name, and articles using various search engines. If you get some hits or indications you have a few choices:

a. Determine whether or not they are used unfairly, or in a way that is unethical or detracts from your mission or product.

b. Determine whether or not the information can be used to your advantage and further your mission or product.

For example, Red Bike Publishing prints government books, documents and regulations. Though they do not write the content, they do professionally design the covers. In some instances, the covers have been used by vendors and other government agencies to further their mission. By default, the cover images are now treated as an industry standard, demonstrating that the image is what the "endorsed" product should look like, and leaving the industry to seek out publications with the image featured on industry leader websites. With that in mind you have a few options:

a.   Contact each website and ask them not to use your image.

b.   Contact each website and ask them to attribute the image to you.

c.   Choose to do nothing and let everyone buy your book. You could blog or write about the success of your book cover and the acceptance within the industry.

Some ways to protect your images is to publish only low-quality images, watermark your company name onto the image on your website, or use software to reform your image into a product box or eBook. However, low-quality images may hurt your marketing.

Summary

Your book helps meet a very important information and training need within your niche. However, your success doesn't have to end with the classes you've created, books you've published or blogs you've maintained. Hopefully, you've been inspired to create spin-off products. Your books should open the door to your online store (website) and your store should point people to your book's point of sale. Keep the momentum going and experiment with different products. Get feedback from your customers and design more spin-off items.

Review Questions

What possible spin-off products related to your book or other products and services can you sell? Answer these questions to find out:

1. Does your specialized market have written guidance or requirements such as state or federal regulations, policy or procedures, or any other publication of rules that you can provide to your customer?

2. Are there study guides, workbooks, training slides or other products you can design related to your book?

3. Can you divide your book in to a portion of its current size and sell it as another book (Part 1 and Part 2 of a title)?

4. Are your books available in both print and as eBooks?

CHAPTER 10 PUTTING IT ALL TOGETHER

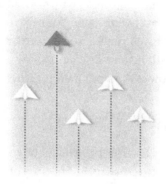

INTRODUCTION

Well, here it is, the ending chapter. It's time to put all of these lessons together and evaluate everything that we've implemented. One thing I've learned in life: A plan is effective until things start moving. That's where life happens and this book is a road map to your book based business success. This chapter will help you evaluate your plan and make adjustments based on your customer's experience.

Congratulations! You are now a successful author and publisher. The press is after you for your story, your friends and family members are carrying you around town on their shoulders, and strangers are buying you dinner...well, not exactly.

Chances are that, outside of your niche, you are barely recognizable. Friends and family don't exactly understand what you are doing, and you barely even get a high five for your efforts. Before you get discouraged about the lack of enthusiasm from those closest to you, let me paraphrase from an ancient writing, "a prophet is without honor in his hometown," or words to that effect. It's not that those you most want to impress don't love you; they really do, but they will not understand how to support you. Your publishing is important to you and your customers, and that relationship is alive and thriving. You might be screaming RECOGNIZE to the wrong crowd. Don't confuse your loved ones' lack of enthusiasm with your ability to meet a market demand; both are differing concepts. Your family loves you for who you are, your market loves you for what you give them. Keeping the correct perspective will resolve grief and allow you to build your niche kingdom. Let's see now how to put it all together.

Keep Websites and Social Media Content Fresh

Let's try something to discover the impact of your website. It's just a small exercise to capture a snapshot in time of your website's performance. To demonstrate this, perform a keyword search for words related to your books and business. Does your website show up in the results? The goal is to have your website featured on the first page of the search results. If it isn't, you may need to do more work.

Once you create your website, be sure to keep the content engaging. After a few months in business, you can discover new information about your book's impact and appeal. While researching your book's performance, put what you've learned on your website to draw even more customers. For example, you may have only received book reviews by a few friends, family, and local book reviewers. Now, after being on the market for a while, new reviews are posted at the online book store pages. Include those reviews on your website and in your marketing plans.

Update the Synopsis

Keep book descriptions alive as you learn from your newsletters, blogs, and customer feedback. In other words, remember the old saying, "Don't rest on your laurels?" Keep getting better and making discoveries about what your audience expresses. A good example of this is that you may have already written your book's description on the published back cover. Since you are both author and publisher, you may have written this in a vacuum, with little outside input. Okay, maybe some friends and family gave halfhearted thumbs up to the description, but you did all the work. In my novel *Commitment - A Novel,* I did the same thing, describing the novel based on what I thought would appeal to readers. Later, I received positive feedback from many readers who shared the many ways the story touched them. These testimonials brought in accounts that had nothing to do with the book's synopsis. I didn't argue with their views or try to "correct" their observations. I shrewdly changed the book's synopsis to capitalize on what I had just learned.

What you originally used to describe your book may evolve into something more meaningful. You might have more of an emotional connection with customers that definitely needs to be reflected on the website. I like to update my website at least monthly as new information gives fresh opportunities for search engines to find my site.

Feed Your Website

Another great way to keep current information flowing is to have your blogs and tweets update and feed into your website every time you post something new (hopefully a few times per week). As you post fresh and exciting information, such as excerpts from your book, positive comments from customers, helpful information related to your books or even information of where your books are sold, they will post to your website. When people search for information with keywords related to your posts, they will be led to your blogs, tweets, and website.

Rename Website Pages

When people search for information, the result is a list of websites with that information either in the title or in the page description. I found that I can get more hits by ensuring the page title contains keywords. If not, you might consider renaming your book's page title. For example, suppose you have a book titled Carrots are Healthy, which describes the many benefits of eating vegetables. The book's page has the notional title of h*ttp://www.mypublishingcompany.com/books/veggiebook*. After doing research, you find that there are many other books about vegetarian food that are getting many more hits. You might find that their pages are *http://www.veggiefood.com*. Do you see the difference in the title string? This happened to one of my books. The keywords were buried in the last part of the title string AND the web address had nothing to do with the book title. Take, for example, a book called NISPOM. My website *www.redbikepublishing.com* is the publishing company, then it is further divided into books or training (*www.redbikepublishing.com/books*). Each of those titles is subdivided into individual book titles or training titles, making the title string longer AND it is mistitled (*www.redbikepublishing.com/books/test-book*). I remedied this by creating a new page just featuring the book title *www.redbikepublishing.com/nispom*. This allowed better placement in search results.

WHAT'S BEST FOR YOU

Don't get tempted to sit back and count on early success. In the same way, don't get discouraged by lack of success. Try new approaches to improve your products and marketing.

When websites, blogs, and social media are set up correctly, niche authors can check marketing statistics regularly and adjust techniques based on the data. That's because online marketing venues provide traffic reports detailing the amount and type of visitors during a selected time frame. These statistics can help determine which articles or blog posts were more effective, where the visitors came from, and how long they stayed. This information is very helpful in determining the best keywords to use to drive traffic to your blogs.

One way to get feedback on website and blog efforts is to track page visits results often and adjust your marketing efforts according to the best reports. Many social media, articles, and blog hosts including Facebook and *ezinearticles.com* provide monthly reporting providing valuable information.

Here's how it might work for you. I write articles that help sell my security books. These articles are primarily featured on my blogs and in *ezinearticles.com*. Ezinearticles.com sends a monthly report that describes activity for the lifetime of the articles I publish. These reports display information regarding the number of times articles were accessed, referenced, and forwarded. I also learn what keywords readers type into search engines to find the articles. Armed with this information, I then incorporate those keywords into future articles and marketing efforts to make them more accessible and increase the marketing footprint.

You May Just Need a Local Printer.

I recently received a phone call from someone asking if Red Bike Publishing, LLC could help get her group's book printed. After a few minutes, I understood that the author wanted to print a specialty book for her small history club. She wanted to print the book, but did not want to make it available online. I quickly realized that the printing and distribution resource my company currently uses would not be a good match for her needs. This was a clue for me to check on other options. In this scenario, bar codes, ISBNs, PCNs and other numbers associated with cataloging and publishing were not needed. She wanted a do-it-yourself book printed whenever she needed it.

Maybe your book project is not necessarily aimed to attract the masses, but just a short term need to train your small groups. Some specific uses include:

- Very few copies for micro use-Members of exclusive clubs and organizations may only require a few copies that are not for the use by or knowledge of non-members. This could include business groups, particularly those working with trade secrets or proprietary information.

•A family tree or honorarium book-Authors want to create a book to honor someone for an accomplishment. Sometimes family members make a "this is your life" book, scrapbook, family history, or retirement gift. No one other than the close family is interested in or needs to know the intimate details.

•Instruction or code of ethics book-Create a means for presenting professional development to a small group. Businesses, organizations, nonprofits, and other entities provide training and instruction on how to perform. Instead of being run through the office copy machine, these products can be raised to the next level with a print quality book. This can include study groups, Sunday classes, tour groups, and much more.

•Customized covers and forewords-Provide your books to several organizations customized for each entity's needs. Groups may request specialized covers. Printing with Ingram Content Group and KDP limits the customization opportunities as each ISBN will only accept one cover and that cover is supplied to the world. It wouldn't help to sell a book on the Internet that is "Customized for Bob." You need another option. If you contract with an independent publisher, they will print on demand and with whatever cover you choose and as many variations as you need. This works well for instances of supplying books to companies with specific messages directed to their employees and the organization's logo captured on the cover.

Finding a private printer is not difficult to do. Just format your book and deliver it to the printer of your choice in the format they work with. Local and national business stores, printing companies, and graphic designers can perform these services. Due to the small amount of books needed, these will be more expensive options. However, the ease of tailoring for specific purposes may be well worth the money. For example, some websites I researched will print a 6x9, 200 page trade book for about $12 if you order twenty copies.

Some other services include poetry and picture books, converting blogs into books, scrapbooks, and other specialty items. Maybe you don't want to provide books to the world, but your books are important nonetheless. That's where specialty printing can help. Use your favorite search engine to find custom book printers. There are so many to choose from that fit your budget and provide exactly what you need.

Prepare For Tax Filing

Writing off expenses is an incredibly helpful way to decrease your tax burden. However, it's not a license to defraud the government. As a rule of thumb, you should claim all of your income and pay what you owe in taxes. In all cases, consult the IRS and a tax accountant as often as necessary. I've found both resources very helpful and patient in leading me through what I thought were difficult questions. The challenge of collecting sales tax and reporting income tax is difficult at first, but it is part of doing business, and is a must for maintaining that business. Failure to do so could result in fines or worse. Doing the right thing will help you better sleep at night, and increase your business savvy.

Income Tax

To file your taxes, you'll need to know all of your sources of income. If printing with KDP, you'll receive a 1099 NEC form at the end of the year. This is comparable to the W2 that employers provide to their employees. Since you as an author or publisher are paid on royalties or products, you will be treated as an independent contractor and will not be treated as an employee. Thus, you will be provided the 1099 MISC and not a W2. As an example, the people running accounts, operating the printing machines, etcetera, are paid employees and will be provided W2s.

If you have set up to do business with these partners, they will have requested that you complete a tax identification number (TIN). The payer will use the TIN information to fill out the 1099 MISC. The 1099 MISC is provided to both the payee and the IRS as reportable income and represents your income from those sources. You will need the 1099 MISC to file your taxes at the end of the year. However, do not forget or neglect to claim your other streams of revenue, such as PayPal, Ingram Content Group, Internet sales, book signings, and other sales revenues. This responsibility to report will rest solely on you as the point of sale, and might require collection of sales tax as well.

Some authors make a lot of money and writing is their only source of income. Some have full time jobs and writing provides some of the household income. Either way, the income made from writing must be claimed during tax time. The only difference is if you have a full time job in addition to writing, your employer is withholding taxes and providing a W2. In your writing business, you should be paying estimated quarterly taxes based on your total income (from a full time job plus other part time jobs, writing, and other sources). What you may not realize is that authors can write off many expenses.

What expenses can be "written off"

There are myriad expenses that authors can write off. However, I would issue a word of caution: Speak with the IRS, state and local sales tax representatives, and tax accountants. The laws are not always clear, so any research you do can only help to solidify your responsibilities while also dispelling any rumors you may be hearing concerning taxes.

I decided to increase my knowledge of what expenses I can write off after going to a new business orientation sponsored by our state and local tax office. The orientation was very helpful, as it allowed me to ask specific questions concerning sales tax, whom I should tax, and how to do so. Though I initially engaged with fear and trepidation, I left with only some frustration about having to pay business privilege tax, but a whole lot of confidence in how to manage sales. This piqued my curiosity to discover what could actually be a write-off expense to lower my tax burden. Since then, I've filed my sales taxes on time and with little difficulty, and have learned what I can do to reduce my tax burden.

Authors can write off anything that justifiably supports the profit making business. Red Bike Publishing, my publishing company, has many moving parts which I have to maintain. Though I've written Get Rich in A Niche to teach publishing and marketing books for little or no expense, there are costs that lead authors to book products that should be tracked and added as expenses during tax filing. These include research, business development, doing business, supplies, and equipment.

Research

I currently have a book idea that is maturing. I've been working on it for about a year and soon will have enough experience and know-how to present this idea as a book. The topic is exercise and how to prepare to be competitive in popular race events called mud runs. In this book, I demonstrate how I was able to shave off six minutes from my performance over five kilometers of mud and obstacles. I also update *http://Runinmud.blogspot.com*, a blog that supports the upcoming book and is packed full of exercises. Hopefully, this book and blog will help people in average physical condition improve their performance and increase their personal record. This type of book requires preparation, going to events, and other research, and that research requires resources. I am keeping track of my fuel, lodging, and other expenses required to make it to the events. These expenses directly impact the book's subject and are related to the research. I also generate an income by selling motivational stickers on *www.cafepress. com/redbikepublishing.*

I also maintain many blogs related to my book topics and the consulting I provide. These topics lead to points of sale and are a result of research. When I spend money and resources on research and can link them to an expense, I will write that expense off. For example, when I do research for *http://jeffsmovieswag.blogspot.com/* my 80s movie review blog, I will write that expense off. For example, if I rent a movie that I intend to review, I can write that off. However, if I take my wife on a date to a recent movie release, I will not write that off. The date and movie topic have nothing to do with the 80s movie reviews. There are also 80s motivational stickers generating income on *www. cafepress.com/redbikepublishing*.

Business Development Costs

In an effort to increase sales, you might have to advertise, join subscription services that manage your communication, set up a booth at a professional conference, join a professional organization, or network to get the word out. These expenses do help generate revenue, but can be deducted as they also chew into your profit. Entertaining clients such as bookstore owners, future authors, or resources for books can be written off as well. You should document these events with dates and receipts and be prepared to show a relationship to your business. You might also account for the cost of attending conferences, giving out review copies of your books, etcetera. After the book is written, authors need a point of sale and this includes website development and hosting. Also, shopping carts are needed and these cost as well. Business cards, marketing efforts, client dinners, and other business development and marketing costs should also be captured.

Cost of Doing Business

Website maintenance, email, newsletter services, advertisement, supplies, and printing costs are just a few costs authors and booksellers may face. Many niche publishers and indie authors market out of their own pockets, using the Internet for points of sale.

Supplies

Paper, pens, pencils, markers, and other expendables associated with your writing should be annotated. These expenses should be tracked and documented for tax returns. Most authors write and store files on the computer. Some actually review and edit those files directly on the computer, however many, like me, actually like to print our writings. I print everything for review and edit many times over. I even print manuscripts exclusively writing for eBook publishing. I print for editing many times over before I even publish them online. One book may produce a few reams of paper before complete and this adds to the cost of supplies. A related expense is printer ink, so don't forget to add it. Fuel is also an expense for business related errands. Be sure to have a log that lists the distance driven and a date, at a minimum. The IRS will give a cost per mile credit of 56.5 cents per mile.

Equipment

Computers, printers, and publishing services are some costs relevant to getting a book to market. These are usually sunken costs that go into preparing a book for market. These expenses can be claimed for tax purposes, both as an expense and as depreciation. Some printers have built in capability to fax, copy, and scan. Be sure to keep receipts for any equipment that you use for book publishing purposes. Post office box fees should be itemized as well.

It's hard enough to make a living writing or running any other type of business. Expenses add up quickly and taxes should be filed on time. The good news is that much of your hard spent expenses can be itemized for tax deduction. This chapter discusses but a few expenses authors can write off. Be sure to check local laws as well as those that allow for deductions. It's worth the effort.

When working on your business, make sure that you are prepared to conduct a lot of administrative tasks. In earlier chapters we talked about scheduling time for writing, but you will also have to take care of the paperwork, to include filing and paying taxes. For federal taxes, this means filing quarterly estimated taxes. This quarterly estimated tax depends on your total income from all sources, including full time jobs and businesses. This tax is also figuring FICA, Medicare, and any profits your business earns (total sales minus expenses).

Sales Tax

Managing taxes is sometimes an easier endeavor when filing as a sole proprietary entity, especially where state jurisdictions are concerned. In these cases, tasks will pull you from your primary business role of writing and publishing to handle mundane but important administrative responsibilities. So, as you form an LLC or other incorporated entity, do your research up front. For example, I just recently converted my business into an LLC. Red Bike Publishing, LLC has a new structure and is expected to maintain that structure according to our State. Tax and business entity rules vary according to where the business is formed as each state has its own requirements. In my state, a business must pay $100 per year, regardless of whether or not the business makes any money. This is called the business privilege tax (BPT). Yes, it's a tax assessed for allowing my company to perform business here.

Red Bike Publishing, LLC only has to pay $100 per year because it does not exceed the multi-million dollar sales threshold. If we did make that kind of money, we would have to pay $200 per year or a percentage of revenue, at least that's how the tax office justified it. Also, LLCs and incorporated business entities must file sales taxes monthly or face a penalty, regardless of whether or not the business actually makes sales within the state. File late and a $50 penalty is incurred. It is the business' responsibility to track sales and collect local and state taxes. For Internet businesses like Red Bike Publishing, LLC, our sales are out of state, but we still have to file "$0.00" or face penalties and fines.

Applicable Sales Tax

As a publisher, you might be set up to do business in state and pay the privilege of doing business tax. Even though you might not have a physical store, your responsibility is to collect state and local taxes from local customers and those located in state. To do this, simply select the sales tax options on your shopping carts or other payment collection options. Some software will allow you to charge varying rates based on selected zip codes. For example, for anyone in my area of zip codes who buys my books online, I must charge county, city, and state taxes. Anyone from outside of the local area, but within the state, is only required to pay state tax. Anyone purchasing from outside of the state does not pay these taxes.

When Not to Pay Sales Tax

If you plan to order books and provide to bookstores within your state or locality, do not charge sales taxes. These taxes should be charged by the resellers to their customers. The same logic applies if providing books to authors for resale. The correct form to use is the Uniform Sales and Use Tax Certificate or equivalent.

Red Bike Publishing, LLC sells primarily through Internet bookstores. These stores are responsible for collecting taxes as customers do not buy from us directly. When we fulfill the orders, we submit them through our printers and distributors (Ingram Content Group and KDP) for print and delivery. The printers charge for the service, print, and deliver to the customer. Recently KDP has charged state sales taxes on orders shipping to certain states. This is because KDP has distribution and printing services in states that charge them sales tax. This sales tax will be charged to the publisher unless the publisher files for exemption with KDP. If the books are going for resale, the cost should be tax exempt. If you fulfill orders yourself through KDP and send orders to a customer, you should be aware of where state taxes apply and factor it into your price for future sales. Again, this can be done through the shopping cart. The other alternative is to not have a point of sale on your website and let Internet stores fulfill all sales.

HOW ABOUT A REWRITE?

Don't let your writing become daunting. Have some fun with it, and when it's not fun, take a break. This might be a good time to leave the new writing and focus on the rewriting season.

I'm using the following approach to update older books on writing, security, and my unpublished novel. Advances in technology, processes, information, and even my own capabilities warrant reassessment and writing updates. Giving your books an update will help boost sales and give you a chance to reintroduce your older products as fresh and revised.

If you already have books available or you have some drafts sitting around, postpone new writing projects and give your old publications a face-lift. Chances are, you might have some work lying around for the past three years that could use some updating. If you have a book, no matter what topic, consider the following four factors and apply them to your niche. For example, I've included examples of how I updated previous versions of this book formerly titled *Get Rich in a Niche*; published way back in 2011. Since then, I've had years of publishing, writing, and blogging experience. Also, publishing processes, technology, and online bookstores have advanced, and it's time for an update.

Ideas for your own rewrites

1. New and more innovative processes are available in your genre. Publishing options have advanced since the last edition. New opportunities to get books out there are now more abundant and there is plenty of positive press for do-it-yourself publishing. As a result of new opportunities, I've included exercises in this edition to help authors determine what type of publishing is right for them.

2. You've become a more accomplished writer with genre material. I've written more blogs explaining the writing and publishing process. With two to three years of additional experience, I can better explain not only the concept of publishing, but application. Now the reader will be more knowledgeable about writing and publishing and they will be equipped to make better decisions.

3. There are more marketing opportunities. Within the past three

years, additional technology, innovation, and know-how is out there to help authors market their books. This makes it possible to add more material to my book, as well as report on what does or doesn't work as well as it used to.

4. You may have more money available to put into your product. When I released Get Rich in a Niche, it was a total grass roots effort. Editing, cover design, and formatting were done with a very limited budget. Now I can afford more professional help and able to outsource important jobs. Rewriting and updates already happening make it the perfect time for an even more professional appearance. Yes, even the novel I've been writing for the past few years is outdated before its release. The technology available to characters has changed from floppy disks to data sticks, and from cordless phones to cell phones. Unless your novel is historical, descriptions of hair and fashion need to be updated to reflect the current era. So, ask yourself the question:

- Does my book need to be updated?

- Have information, technology, products or processes changed enough to warrant a rewrite?

- Have my skills improved enough to put out a better product?

If the answers are yes, consider spending the next few months to a year rewriting your books and updating the spin-off products.

WHERE TO PUT YOUR MONEY

Okay, so the premise of this book is free marketing. I'm still claiming that free marketing strategies are the most effective. But here is where I start talking about spending money on enabling your business. Don't confuse spending money on enabling your business with paid advertising. What I am suggesting is that once you begin to make money, you will discover that the free marketing efforts are very effective, while your ability to continue the high performance marketing tasks becomes less effective.

Marketing takes time. I've discovered that the more books I write, the more authors I take on, and the more rewriting that needs to be conducted, and my time becomes even more divided. So what's an entrepreneur to do? Go find some other entrepreneurs to take over some tasks.

Fortunately for niche authors working on a budget, there are also some niche entrepreneurs operating on similarly tight budgets but with reasonable costs. True, there are those who will edit your books, design covers, and offer publicity services each costing thousands of dollars. Their time and effort is very much worth the cost. However, unless you plan to sell a lot of books, you can't afford the investment. If you can sell a lot of books to justify the expense, go for it.

At this point, I would like to define the phrase "meaningful budget". As with any program, you want to meet schedule, performance, and cost requirements. Get your publications out on time, keep information accurate, cutting edge, and entertaining, and make a profit. Each requirement must balance. If you don't get your book out as scheduled, you'll miss an opportunity to sell. If your book has low quality information and packaging, you won't sell many books. If you exceed costs while ensuring schedule and performance, you will sell your books at a loss. Meaningful budget means meeting all three requirements. Publish your book within the meaningful budget parameters.

As my publishing services grow, I meet more people who are capable, hungry for work, and charge a reasonable rate. In the beginning, even a few hundred bucks would break my bank. However, as I plug along, I can add the cost of doing good business to my budget. I happily bring capable people on my team. Though not full time employees, I give them work on a case by case basis and issue each a form 1099 MISC at the end of the year. I can tell you that my life is so much better knowing that my editing, cover designs, and marketing are outsourced and performing at a level way higher than I could ever do myself; these folks have real talent and a love of their work. I'm so glad to have them in my life so I can focus on writing. If you want to know who I use, please see the acknowledgments at the beginning of this book.

Cover design. I used to design my own covers, now I use *99designs. com*. This website allows clients to describe their design needs and does well matching up clients with designers. You can hire designers directly or start a design contest, get many cover designs, and pick your choice. I've had many covers designed for under $300.

Editing. Even though I write, edit, and rewrite many times, there will be tons of mistakes that I never catch. Friends and family members also provide help, but they often don't have the skills to catch them all. Now I outsource editing to someone who is so well educated and that knowledge is ingrained in her DNA, so much so that she can't help but find grammatical errors and misspellings everywhere. You need someone like that on your team. I've put her contact information in the front matter of this book if you are interested in contacting her. Now, our products are levels above what they used to be, thanks to her skills and, again, love of her work. If you can afford professional editing and stay within a meaningful budget, I highly recommend it.

There it is, the end of the book, for now. So let's talk about you. Your adventure is underway, so experience it. Control what you can control to make sure your customers are able to find the great information you provide and acquire it easily. There are probably many ideas and methods you have personally discovered that work well for you, but are not mentioned in this book. I applaud your creativity and would love to hear what you have learned.

Until then, keep learning and creating.

APPENDIX A

Here is your chance to set your plan to become a niche expert. In the requirement column, put your goal. For example, you might determine that you need a blog to reach more people. Place "create a blog" under the Requirement header. Under the Action header, you would write find a blog host, register for blog, create a blog name and write articles.

Requirement	Action		

APPENDIX B

Spin-off ideas may be spontaneous. On your journey to become a niche expert, you might discover some product ideas. As you write your book, blog, ezine articles, or interact with your customer base, you may discover needs not being met. You can keep track of those ideas with Niche Market Spin-off Idea tracking sheet.

Niche Title	Published Book Title	Regulations or Guidelines?	Spin-off Product 1	Spin-off Product 2	Spin-off Product 3	Spin-off Product 4

APPENDIX C

Use the Niche Market Spin-off Idea Detail Sheet to create a product marketing plan.

Niche Market Spin-off Idea
Idea:
Reason:
Strong selling point 1:
Strong selling point 2:
Strong selling point 3:
Strong selling point 4:

ABOUT THE AUTHOR

As a niche leader, Jeffrey W. Bennett has written and published many niche books with his company Red Bike Publishing. Jeff is a former Army officer and speaks three languages. He has an M.B.A. from Columbia College and a Masters Degree in Acquisitions and Procurement Management from Webster University.

Jeff created a niche industry from his first book ISP Certification, which is a study guide for security professionals. From there, he has written books and training and created a six figure business. He likes to show people how he did it.

Jeff is a featured speaker at many venues including the University of Alabama in Huntsville and is on call to write articles for national magazines and blogs. Jeff is a regular contributor to www.*clearancejobs.com*.

To find out more about him, visit:

www.jeffreywbennett.com

Jeff also offers security, writing and publishing courses at:

www.bennettinstitute.com

Hear Jeff's Podcasts:
Security: *www.redbikepublishing.com/dodsecure*
Book Based Business Incubator:
https://www.redbikepublishing.com/start-business-podcast/

ABOUT THE PUBLISHER

Mission:
Red Bike Publishing exists to create value for our partners, shareholders, and customers by building a business to last.

As the preeminent niche publishing organization, we offer what other publishers cannot: focused delivery of industry publications to enhance the professional's skill level. We do this by writing and publishing superior nonfiction, traditional, and eBooks, and by providing empowering training resources at affordable prices.

Vision:
Red Bike Publishing will be valued for our one-of-a-kind niche publishing and the ability to positively impact our customers.

Books

Our books are available on Amazon.com and other online book stores. Our website also sells books at *https://www.redbikepublishing.com.*

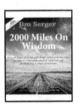

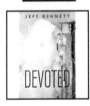

Training

Book Based Business Incubator Training:

https://bennettinstitute.com/course/book-based-business-incubator/

A special word of thanks

Thank you for ordering my book. I really appreciate you and hope you are able to apply what you learned here to create your own business based on your niche book.

If you are able to, feel free to tell me about how you are going to use your knowledge. You can email me at: editor@redbikepublishing.com

I would really love to hear your feedback and your input would help to make the next version of this book and my future books better.

Please leave a helpful review on Amazon letting others know what you thought of the book.

You can review here https://www.amazon.com/review/create-review/?ie=UTF8&channel=glance-detail&asin=B0056QJKFE

A gift for you

I also have a gift for you. I have a downloadable workbook with all the tables available at:

www.redbikepublishing.com/nicheworkbook

Thanks so much

Jeff